LAST DRINK TO LA

LAST DRINK TO LA

JOHN SUTHERLAND

✳ **SHORT BOOKS**

FRONT LINES

First published in 2001 by
Short Books
15 Highbury Terrace
London N5 1UP

A CIP catalogue record for this book
is available from the British Library.

ISBN 0 571 20855 X

Printed in Great Britain by
Bookmarque Ltd, Croydon, Surrey

I GOT DRUNK in many places and got sober in Los Angeles – with the help of Alcoholics Anonymous. I no longer reside permanently in Los Angeles County and am no longer a regular attender of AA meetings. Nor, in writing this, can I claim to have safeguarded my anonymity, as conscientious members of the fellowship are enjoined to.

I am not drinking just now. Nor have I drunk alcohol for almost two decades (five undergraduate degrees, three PhDs, four Californian marriages, and two life-sentences, as I like to calculate). I abhor the preferred AA term for sober initiates – 'recovering alcoholic' – which has to my ear a Uriah Heepish ring. I prefer to think of myself as 'past it'; over that hill, a *veterano*, as the Hispanics (who honour such oldsters) say. And, I will confess, I am no longer up to the strenuous physical demands of booze. 'Serious' drinkers, as they jestingly call themselves, enjoy a longer career than football players, but not much. 'Practising' (as opposed to 'recovering') alcoholism is not for weaklings. Books are easier.

For what it is worth, this book is a meditation. It is not a temperance tale ('How I Conquered the Demon Rum'). Nor is it a treatise on the disease of alcoholism (if one is wanted, I would recommend *Alcoholism* by Neil Kessel and Henry Walton; it used to be available as a Penguin but will now have to be hunted down second-hand). Least of all is this what AA calls a 'drunkalog' – or drunkard's exemplary tale ('How the Demon Rum Conquered Me') – told to terrify, inform and instruct. Just some thinking about drinking.

The Drinking Life (and Death)

Some would say (certainly many members of AA) that only those who have plumbed the abyss will ever know the huge semantic gaps that lie between the simple sentences 'I have drunk', 'I am drunk' and 'I am a drunk'. Least of all do the white-coated 'experts' know. In this area of medical research only the guinea pigs wear the white coats; they alone are expert. For myself, I used to drink, as they say, 'like a fish' (except, as I understand it, fish don't drink, any more than the maligned newt inebriates himself). Drink practically killed me – as it actually kills hundreds of thousands of my drunken fellow-citizens every year.

It would have been of no great moment had I drunk

myself to death in the early 1980s, the climacteric of my drinking career. There would have been no banner announcements or half-page obituaries in the press; no solemn minute of silence in my employing institution (although I believe, as a 'Reader in English', I would have warranted a day's half-mast of the college flag at UCL). As far as the world was concerned, the demise of Sutherland would have been just another sot gone to his liquid grave.

There are, by modest calculation, a hundred such deaths a day (three times the daily number of deaths by road accidents; innumerably more than are stabbed, strangled or shot to death in the UK). The response of those bereaved of my presence would have been one of discreetly masked relief. Whatever there was to lose had been lost ('pissed away', as they say) years ago. Money, trust, houses, job, marriage, liver, lights and lungs. Above all – respect. There are many Shakespearean lines that resonate for drunks, but none more so than Othello's agonised adieu to the world's admiration:

> O, now, for ever
> Farewell the tranquil mind! farewell, content!
> Farewell the plumèd troops and the big wars
> That make ambition virtue!

There are, by official estimate, some 300,000 lives terminated or shortened by alcohol abuse in the UK every year.

Society at large is admirably stoical about this annual Passchendaele, as it is about the fewer (but still staggeringly numerous) citizens who wipe themselves out on the roads, day in, day out. People must travel; people must drink; fish gotta swim.

Often, of course, the two bills of mortality converge: alcohol is reckoned to be a factor in over 50 per cent of automobile crashes – particularly after the pubs and bars close and the A&E rooms move on to red-alert for the nocturnal *tsunami* of blood, liquor and petroleum spirit that washes into the country's hospitals. Among those waiting for treatment will be a sizable number of sober victims of alcohol: 40 per cent of violent crime and 90 per cent of assaults in Britain are recorded as being 'alcohol-related'. Cheers.

According to Alcohol Concern's latest spoilsport bulletin, three out of four British adults have had their lives severely disrupted by their own or someone else's alcohol abuse. And what does that bleak Latinism 'disruption' mean? Blood, bruises, scratches, curses, screams.

In October 2000, the sociologist Betsy Stanko took a 'snapshot' of domestic violence in Britain and came up with the headline-grabbing statistic that there were, over the course of any day, an average of 600 'incidents' an hour. Some 570,000 acts of domestic violence are reported each year in Britain, and many more, given the behind-doors nature of the offence, elude official notice. Alcohol figures in most of these invisible crimes. The sober thump is, apparently, a rarity.

It needs, as Horatio would say, no sociologist to tell us these things. *Circumspice*; drink's monuments are everywhere around us. Alcoholism is immensely destructive. And expensive. Every few months some committee or other will tot up the zillions it costs the country in road accidents, premature death, burden on the health service, family breakdown, suicide, homicide, assault, bankruptcy, homelessness, police, probation and court time.

Why do you drink? the Little Prince asks the drunkard. Because I am unhappy, the drunkard replies. Why are you unhappy? Because I drink.

In the face of this carnage and misery, society displays an amazing degree of Alcohol Unconcern. Abuse is serenely tolerated. If a pretender to the premiership boasts, as a lad, to have drunk 14 pints, or the current premier's son is found paralytic after his many pints in Leicester Square, it is thought of as no more than a manly rite of passage. Beer Street is as wholesomely British as it was in Hogarth's day; not so Drug Lane.

The damage to the social fabric attributable to alcohol is, however vast, a bearable cost. It is not 'tragedy' but 'statistics' – as Stalin dismissively said of his millions of soldiers dying on the Eastern Front. Sticks and stones can break our bones but numbers can never hurt us. Even eight-digit numbers. The cost of alcohol is a domestic price that liberal Western democracies, for all their squeamishness about hanging murderers and priggishly 'ethical' foreign policies, have always been willing for their peoples to pay. Eager even.

What does society get in return for the licence it grants its citizens to intoxicate and immolate themselves? At some deep Machiavellian level, the incessant, society-wide overdose of alcohol is, one presumes, prescribed (or at least condoned) by our leaders as something prophylactic. Chronic drunkenness inhibits reasoned protest, organised resistance – even revolution, if that's the flavour of the time. 'Let them lick the sweet that is their poison', as Coriolanus says of the Roman plebeians. Rome will be that much more easily governed by the patriciate if the *canaille* are so occupied.

To think thus may be paranoia – as whites thought it paranoiac that African-Americans should allege that the CIA flooded big-city ghettoes with narcotics in the 1970s to exterminate Black Pride, Black Consciousness and (most effectively) Black Power. 'Hey, hey! You can buy your gage from the CIA' sings the dissident West Side rapper Ice Cube. He means now.

Paranoid it may be but I *do* think that the government's

toleration of alcohol abuse (an 'issue' which they could as easily 'address' as fox-hunting) is motivated, at least in part, by Coriolanian cynicism. Let them swig the sweet that is their poison; a pissed electorate is (politically) a docile electorate, except, predictably, on Saturday nights and at big football matches – 'hooligan' outbursts which the Home Secretary can handle with his big stick, and, if not, let's vote in the Tories with their bigger stick. I also half-credit Ice Cube's allegations about the CIA pushing crack to ghetto kids in South Central. After all vodka and acquiescence to tyranny are intimately linked in 20th-century Russian history. Picture the future, O'Brien tells Winston Smith in *Nineteen Eighty-four*: a boot stamping on a human face for ever. Alcohol numbs the pain of the tyrant's boot. For ever, it seems.

Unlike other opiates of the people, alcohol does not tranquillise – but it does deaden reason (listen to the late-night conversation in any bar). Drunkenness stimulates violent but wholly thoughtless action. The routine red-mist/blackout defence in alcoholic crimes of passion is: 'I don't know what came over me.' It's usually true. 'Why are you looking for your keys here when you dropped them over there?' the policeman asks the drunk. 'Because here is where the streetlamp is,' replies the drunk. The alcoholic mind at work.

The other signal difference between alcohol and narcotics is that drinking to drunkenness and 'incapability' (unlike the high that comes with a heroin hit or cocaine snort) takes several hours to be successfully achieved. And, unlike hard drugs, it can be continued for decades at toxic levels of intake before the organism gives way. Drinking gives the people (particularly young, dangerous males) something to do with their leisure time and most rebellious years. Until, that is, they become civilised. Or, at least, tired and law-abiding.

Because of what it does to their brains and their reputations, drinkers (unlike, say, people with Aids or even pot-heads), are never capable of organising themselves as a 'lobby' or interest group. No one speaks for them (although many speak at and about them – the madwomen of Mothers Against Drunken Drivers (MADD) and the prigs at Alcohol Concern, for example). 'Petrol protests', however illogical, selfish and thoughtless about the global environment, can attract moral support from the amoral majority, righteously indignant at 'stealth taxes'. But to protest at the sky-high (and rising) 'sin tax' on alcohol is to argue oneself sinful. (I have always believed that the dramatic revival of the Scottish National Party's fortunes in the 1970s had much to do with the party's rash promise to lower the price of a bottle of whisky to 60p.)

Every month or so newspapers dust off their 'alcohol

epidemic' story or column. It invariably takes the same shock-horror form. Typically, the tone is gothic, designed to reassure the drinking reader that he/she is not *so* far gone and never will be.

I take the following, at random, from the *Independent*, 11 November 2000. Fergal Keane (a BBC special correspondent) is writing an 'op-ed' piece about the drink 'n' drugs death of the celebrity Paula Yates (the result of a 'foolish' overdose, the coroner declared):

> I've seen more than a few friends die from addiction, and I lost a parent to the disease. It is closer to me in my daily life as both legacy and living issue than anything. When I write about it, I struggle to step back and see things in anything like cold light. So forgive me if it reads like I'm losing the plot here. I don't have an ounce of distance in me when it comes to this stuff.
>
> And so I feel a quiet rage when I see how so much of the media distorts the truth of addiction. I watch the replays of Oliver Reed and George Best disintegrating drunk on television and feel sick in my stomach. Here are men killing themselves while we are urged to celebrate their wildness. Would we stick cancer victims on prime-time and then replay the tapes endlessly for our enjoyment? It is as if there is no connection whatsoever between the wild man antics – 'magnificent', I heard one chat-show host call Reed – and the

shivering figures pissing blood in the dawn as their livers disintegrate.

Powerful stuff. But who are the 'we', Fergal? As the same edition of the *Independent* proudly records, its daily circulation has risen to 240,407 (the highest figure for three years). Surveys routinely reveal that in advanced and prosperous Western societies, some ten per cent of the population – irrespective of class – will be damaged by their drinking practices; whether habitual, recreational or occasional. This means (assuming, conservatively, two readers a copy) some 48,000 of 'us' *Independent* readers are up there every dawn with the blood-pissers. Enough to fill an Olympic-sized swimming pool and do one's morning laps.

That ten per cent is food for thought, if we cared to think about it. It means that every tenth person you pass on the street (or, terrifyingly, every tenth driver who streaks past you in the fast lane) will be a 'problem drinker' (another strange locution; if only one could drink one's problems, eat one's debts and excrete moderation).

As Dylan Thomas wisecracked, an alcoholic is someone you don't like who drinks as much as you do. For the British press, an alcoholic is someone who drinks *even* more than you, but of whom – like the Pharisee – you can (just about) say, 'Thank God I am not as that man is; well, not *quite* as that man is.'

To shock without being a killjoy requires a delicate professional hand. Fortunately, the practising (but 'denying') alcoholics who read newspapers are as adept at wilful doublethink as are journalists in skilful doublespeak. Alcoholic Calibans specialise in not seeing their image, but that of an ugly *other* Caliban, in the handmirror. It goes with those other alcoholic skills; what in AA-speak is called 'powerful forgetting' (convenient repression of uncomfortable facts) and 'screwy thinking' (paranoia, typically, but sometimes compulsive obsessive disorder, the flavour-of-the-month malady in the US, or suicidal melancholia).

Journalists are, of course, like publicans and servicemen, an 'at risk' profession. But so are most professions. Some social groups seem less prone than others to problem drinking: the Irish, Scots and Scandinavians are notoriously prone; Jews and Sikhs less so. But, as any AA group witnesses, alcohol, like cancer, is a great leveller and can leap any class and ethnic boundaries.

Its leaps are getting longer. AA members used to be middle-aged by and large. 'It takes a lot of years to get sober' was the grey-headed wisdom of the meetings (AA is as addicted to the pithy proverb as to stewed coffee). Nowadays, the fellowship is typically younger; particularly in metropolitan America. The reasons? The erosion of licensing laws and unenforced age-limits; huge amounts of disposable income released into young pockets by the bullish 1990s stock market, the economic boom and the IT revolution; stronger beers; the vogue for liquor-based cocktails (as in that other 'roaring' decade, the 1920s); and, above all, multi-drug abuse.

Using, say, marijuana or cocaine in combination with alcohol produces an accelerator effect. It may be chemical or a consequence of social disinhibition (using an illegal substance plausibly encourages less controlled use of the legal substance). Who knows? But, observably, two-fisted addicts fall faster and harder.

There are, it has to be said, nobler reasons for drinking than that of Saint-Exupéry's sad sack and his whingeing 'because I'm unhappy'. My favourite *apologia pro vita alcoholica sua* is Jack London's in *John Barleycorn*. He drank, the wolf-lover loftily proclaimed, to make other (sober) people interesting. It's a gallant thought. Nor is it uncommon, hollow as London's gallantry may ring in the sober ear. The film star George Sanders, a sad and sodden late-life drunk, topped himself – after a long career playing drawling *ennuyés* – with the bleak suicide note for posterity, 'You bore me so.' Let's hope he's having a livelier time in drunk's heaven, that big rock-candy mountain in the sky.

Finding your sober *semblables* and *frères* so boring

that they drive you to drink is the last high ground left to the drunk. They (we) are so *dull*. It's not very elevated but, like blind Gloster's hillock in *King Lear*, any eminence will do for alcoholic suicide. (Jack London killed himself – impulsively, and with a narcotic; unable to put up any longer with the intolerable boredom of life among the sober, presumably.)

In *A Drinking Life*, Pete Hamill's tough, but sensitive journalist's memoir of alcoholism and recovery (sans AA, allegedly), he discovered the root reason he drank when he saw Norman Mailer, drunk and pathetic, make a fool of himself at a riotous party. Unable to stand the sight of his hero being laughed at, Hamill rushed out into the New York street:

> I walked for blocks, suddenly understanding clearly that another of the many reasons I drank was to blur the embarrassment I felt for my friends. If a friend was drunk and making an ass of himself, then I'd get drunk and make an ass of myself too. And there was some residue in me of the old codes of the Neighborhood, some deep adherence to the rules about never, ever rising above your station. Getting drunk was a way of saying I would never act uppity, never forget where I came from. No drunk, after all, could look down on others. Being drunk was the great leveller, a kind of Christian act of communion. Who could ever point the

finger at a drunk if *all* were drunk? I'd do the same thing in the company of friends who thought they were failures and I was a success. Who could accuse me of snobbery, a bighead, deserting my friends, if I was just another bum in the men's room throwing up on his shoes.

There are other, equally riddling replies to the Little Prince's question. 'Why do you drink?' – 'I drink to forget.' 'To forget what?' – 'I can't remember.' One takes refuge in smart replies because straight answers are extremely hard to come up with.

Most drunks have been asked, typically amid some spectacular wreckage of their lives: why the *hell* do you do it? At such desperate moments, the teenage killers Leopold and Loeb's defiantly Nietzschean answer appeals: 'Because I *damn* well want to.'

But many don't want to. Like D.H. Lawrence's horse on the verge of bolting, they have two wills; and the will to drink is stronger than that to stop. After a certain point, internal resistance crumbles. The drunk can no more stop drinking destructively than the suicide who has thrown himself out of a skyscraper can stop falling. The best he can manage is the falling man's jaunty 'so far so good'. Optimists that they are, AA alcoholics like to picture their descent as more like that of sinking gently through fathoms of water like Ferdinand's father; when the bottom is touched, they will rise again to the air – DV. The bard himself, folklore has it, died of drink.

A few are saved; most are destroyed or badly damaged. The odds against healthy survival are no secret. Why then drink to destruction? Every swallow is a willed, deliberate act. Very little alcohol is given away (never enough for the serious drinker). Alcoholism is the sum result of millions of voluntary decisions and purchases. It's mysterious. Particularly so at the beginning of a drinking career, when one still has choices and can clearly foresee outcomes and plan one's game. Why, as Cassio plaintively asks in *Othello* – amid the debris of his ruined army career – do men put thieves in their mouths to steal out their brains? Why do they *pay* to do it; not just with money, but (if push comes to shove) with every possession that can be pawned to get more drink? The answer that many drunks would be inclined to give, if it didn't seem flippant, is that it feels good and seems right at the time. Or, as the more mature drunk, further into his career, might say: 'It *used* to feel good, and I want – I need – that feeling again.'

Alcoholic pleasure is described as something erotic – orgasmic, even – in Caroline Knapp's hypersensitive journalist's memoir, *Drinking: A Love Story*.

A love story. Yes: this is a love story. It's about passion, sensual pleasure, deep pulls, lust, fears, yearning hungers. It's about needs so strong they're crippling. It's about saying good-bye to something you can't fathom living without.

I loved the way drink made me feel; and then loved its special power of deflection; its ability to shift my focus away from my own awareness of self and on to something else, something less painful than my own feelings. I loved the sounds of drink: the slide of a cork as it eased out of a wine bottle, the distinct glug-glug of booze pouring into a glass, the clatter of ice cubes in a tumbler. I loved the rituals, the camaraderie of drinking with others, the warming, melting feelings of ease and courage it gave me.

The primal bliss about which Knapp rhapsodises is short-lived and not, alas, easily recaptured. And, with time (as 'tolerance' builds), the intake required for what Tennessee Williams calls the 'click' is so numbingly high that feeling anything other than a persistent ache in the bladder (and later the head) is a daunting challenge. But one chases it, *ignis fatuus*, or not, until the swamp closes over one's head.

Tolerance initially feels good: you can 'hold your drink' (more importantly, hold your job, hold your marriage together). To drink and never to get drunk is the mid-career drunk's proudest achievement – paradoxical as it seems. One of my favourite scenes of this alcoholic chauvinism is in the not very distinguished 1961 film *The*

Comancheros (directed by Michael Curtiz). John Wayne (white hat) and Lee Marvin (black hat) are, for their respective ends, both pretending to be staggering drunk. Both have consumed, we apprehend, many shots (bottles, even) of rotgut whisky (no sarsparilla for these tough guys). In fact, they are both stone-cold sober, testing each other out.

For alcoholics (ten per cent of the audience, to be tediously repetitious), the reassuring element in the drinking-but-not drunk scene is that 'serious drinkers', manly drinkers like our heroes (and ourselves), can 'hold' the booze. Bacchus wins no easy victory over these topers. Or us. Off-stage, in real life, both actors were known to be heroic drinkers; something that added savour to the scene on-screen.

Marvin died wretchedly from his disease. Wayne was saved from a wet death by the lung cancer which suffocated him (heroic in everything, the Duke claimed to have smoked 100 cigarettes a day and, after having one dead lung removed, declared that he had 'licked cancer').

Tolerance, alas, does not last. After a few years of being steeped in it, alcohol (like other addictive drugs) reverses on you. Damn it. It's not that you feel good when you imbibe, you feel bad when you don't. At the very end of the line you need drink medicinally to allay the pains ('withdrawal') of abstinence. Sobriety, not over-indulgence, has now become your ailment. Intoxication is the only cure for the toxin of alcohol. Alcoholism, in its final stages, is quaintly homeopathic. You need a 'hair of the dog'; antidote alcohol to counteract the poison, which is – alcohol, of course.

Tolerance wilts, in the last stages of alcoholism, under the grossly anaesthetic amount of drink needed to keep pain at bay. And, at the end of the road, tolerance goes altogether. One drink will do what a bottle used to. One is back where one started; but without the primal joy that kicked the whole cycle off. It is no longer a 'love story'.

I daresay some ingenious alcoholic has set up an IV drip to maintain the alcohol level in the blood during sleep. But most drunks – however far along the arc – abstain when unconscious, setting in train the torments of 'withdrawal' – hangover, as it is called.

All alcoholics start the day with headaches, nausea and anorexia. Enough to take the sober citizen immediately to the casualty ward. One of the sharpest descriptions of hangover that I know is in a neglected novel, *The Morning After*, by Jack Wiener. The hero, a Los Angeles PR man, Chuck Lester, wakes in a hotel after a night on the razzle. He has asked for an early call – he has an important morning meeting:

My mouth was caked and parched, my throat was sore. Probing with my tongue, I felt bits of sour undigested food. I had vomited in my sleep. The pillow was wet beneath my cheek, sticky. Raising my head abruptly, pain shot through my skull, forcing me down. But the odour was too strong. I became nauseous. I couldn't stand, had to crawl to the toilet on my hands and knees.

Empty, my eyes watering, I stretched out on the cool tile floor. I fought to rise. I'd have to strip the bed. But I couldn't get up. Each time I raised my head the pain stabbed across my temples.

What time? I lifted my arm to look at my watch. Unable to focus at first. Bringing it closer, squinting. Ten after eight. *No. It couldn't* be; she was supposed to call at seven. I looked again. It was true; ten after eight. Christ, she never called. The stupid rotten bitch had never called.

I was due to meet Rudy in 40 minutes. I had to shower and shave and dress. Clean up the mess, get some coffee down. Be presentable and alert. Articulate.

What the hell was I going to *do*? Idiot. Stupid, fucking idiot.

Panic-stricken, I lay there, immobile. Staring at a tiny crack in the ceiling. I could call, say that I was sick, had sprained my ankle. Slash my wrists in a bathtub of warm water. Help me, God help me. Please.

Wiener's description of the condition is so painfully accurate that one could assume he may be a fellow-sufferer. He is also clearly a Los Angeles man. I looked hopefully for him at every meeting I went to where a speaker said: 'My name is Jack. I'm an alcoholic.' No luck.

When one wakes with a real hangover, forget coffee. Only a 'phlegm-cutter' (George V. Higgins's wonderfully graphic term) will still the shakes, calm the morning panic, keep at bay the terrors. Delirium tremens, the final collapse of consciousness into hallucination under the stress of withdrawal, is, typically, a disease of the early morning.

DTs is nothing like the 'pink elephant' fantasia in Walt Disney's film, *Dumbo*. A graphic description is given by Charles Jackson in *The Lost Weekend* (it was somewhat tidied up in Billy Wilder's film version; Wilder also latched an optimistic ending on to Jackson's bleakly pessimistic fable of the drinking life). Don Birnam, in the novel's presentation, has come to the end of a long drunk. He is now dry and in terminal withdrawal. A small friendly mouse (as he perceives) has burrowed its way out of the wall and is looking at him. He feels, like Robbie Burns, a fellowship with the poor cowering beastie. Suddenly a bat flutters past and springs on to the mouse:

> The obscene wings hid how the contest went. They were folded around the opening of the hole, hooked into the plaster, deathly still; they stirred with a scratching sound as

the bat shifted for position. There was a smell. His breath stopped in his agony to see. The wings spread as the bat began to squeeze the small bat body of the mouse – he could see the gripping claws like miniature nail-parings. The horrible wings lifted, the round ears of the bat disappeared, as its teeth sank into the struggling mouse. The more it squeezed, the wider and higher rose the wings, like tiny filthy umbrellas, grey-wet with slime... Tiny drops of bright blood spurted down the wall; and from his bed he heard the faint miles-distant shrieks of dying.

One of the more ingenious literary treatments of the DTs is in Kingsley Amis's ghost story, *The Green Man*. Amis's hero, Maurice Allington, suffers from alcohol-induced jactitation (convulsive twitching) and hypnagogic hallucinations (as did Amis). But, at the same time, Maurice is haunted. Which is the supernatural and which the alcoholic spectre? Supposing Macbeth (like too many other Scots) was a heavy drinker: what would one make then of the dagger he sees before him? ('Cut back on the usquebaugh, laddie.')

My own brush with the DTs was more banal. On one occasion, I was convinced that there was someone (it might, in point of fact, have been a giant toad), just outside my field of vision, about to pounce. On another, I recall turning a number of pictures to the wall to stop them staring. Nothing quite as horrific as what Birnam/Jackson evidently experiences.

The pictures also, as I recall, spoke to me. 'Voices' are a less florid hallucination, which afflicts terminal drunks in extreme withdrawal. Typically, the voices are less heard than dimly overheard – coming out of cold-water taps, through the central heating, or (in my case) electric kettles and hanging pictures. And, typically, they are overheard saying bitchy things about one (eavesdroppers, of course, never hear good things about themselves). Sometimes as strangers pass in the street, they will be 'heard' – by the deluded alcoholic ear – muttering some barely audible insult. Many a pointless brawl has been started that way.

Evelyn Waugh, an alcohol and chloral abuser, wrote an amusing novel around these voices (which the author had experienced himself, during a spectacular late-life breakdown). In *The Ordeal of Gilbert Pinfold* (or 'Portrait of the Artist in Middle-Age'), the hero (Waugh to the life) embarks on an ocean cruise to recover his health. He hears a series of conspiratorial conversations, relayed – as he deludedly thinks – through the ship's air vents: 'I don't say he's an actual card-carrying member of the Communist Party,' one voice says, 'but he's certainly mixed up with them.' 'Most Jews are,' another voice answers. And so it goes – Kurt Vonnegut's catchphrase, a writer who has clearly done research into the rituals of AA to judge by the 'Serenity Prayer' with which he chose to conclude *Slaughterhouse-Five*.

Once the drinker has experienced DTs and heard those vaguely persecuting voices, madness ('wet brain') and other kinds of serious organic decay are imminent. The end is nigh. Drink and die, or stop. Most don't.

None the less, the quest for joy remains to the end. There was a time – now long forgotten – when even the skid-row drunkard drank because it made him merry and life look good. That mirage is pursued. Even as the last months of their pathetic lives run out, you see a group of winos in the park: men (usually) who have manifestly lost everything. They are disgustingly unkempt and can be smelled at ten paces if you are injudicious enough to come that close. They have not, probably, long to live and that little time will be uncomfortable. All that holds their *posse comitatus* together is the brown-bagged bottle, or can, which they pass and swig (unwiped) from hand to mouth to hand to mouth. Passers-by will hear their rambling, slurred, periodical ranting or lachrymose, too-loud discourse punctuated by gales of raucous laughter.

What do these wrecks have to laugh about? Being relieved of the need to work – and the disturbing fact that (as Steve Martin wryly pointed out) they tend to have good heads of hair – is all that makes these deadbeats enviable to their sober, industrious, world-fearing fellow-citizens. (On the hair: is never shampooing the secret (as Martin muses)? Or are the moulting strands stuck to their heads by the adhesive goo that oozes from their scalps?) Whatever the weather, park drunks seem, like the monkeys in the zoo, to be having fun; at least intermittently. No one else in the park is laughing uproariously.

Alcohol, viewed objectively, is no fun whatsoever. The social life of the far-gone drunk is Sartrean in its loneliness. Alcohol-abuse features, often as the primary cause, in many divorce cases. But the alcoholic will probably be disjoined from more than the bone of his bone, flesh of his flesh. At the end of the road, he has no colleagues, no *fidus achates*, no 'community care'. If he has a dog to share his blanket, or his cardboard box, one has to wonder at canine irrationality (as when Bull's Eye follows his psychopathic master, Bill Sikes, to destruction). But at least four-legged friends are not so irrational as to drink (the only alcoholic dog I know of in literature is Rum Dum in Nelson Algren's *Man with the Golden Arm*). Drunkenness is the main cause of 'homelessness' – as street destitution and vagrancy are euphemistically called. At least lepers had colonies. The homeless sleep as solitary as Crusoe on his island.

Lonely as the sufferer will be, alcoholism is, in its effect, the least self-contained of afflictions. Cancer, even HIV, you can keep to yourself, but not diseases of the bottle. Sooner or later, you will be outed and cast out by your sober fellows. 'Secret drinker' is, for career-drinkers, a contradiction in terms. The habit, once it takes hold, cannot be kept under wraps. The domestic fallout of alcoholism can trickle down for generations in the form of financial, social or emotional ruin. Grossly unfair as it is, the innocent partners and offspring of the drunkard will share the stigma; social, moral and psychological. George Cruikshank's *The Drunkard's Children* is, with its innocent victims, a more pathetic series of plates by far than his *The Bottle*. The alcoholic's thoughtless bequest to his loved ones rivals anything a sadist might invent.

Save yourself is the bleak advice usually given to those with an unregenerate drunk in the family. Pack your bag, scoop up the kids, raid the piggy-bank, leave and don't look back. There are few more pathetic 12-step gatherings than those of the Adult Children of Alcoholic Parents, Al-Anon (for partners and family), or Al-Ateen (for adolescent children of alcoholics). Those who have stayed on, cohabiting with a drunk out of residual love, loyalty or financial dependency have a hard time of it. Like syphilis in an Ibsen play, it poisons families incurably, generation after generation.

The favoured prescription in American counselling circles now is the 'early intervention' – a 'nipping in the bud', 'stitch in time saves nine' measure. Intervention normally takes the form of an ultimatum, delivered *ensemble* by the drinker's family. Typically, the alcoholic is surprised by the confrontation. You come home, perhaps after a night on the batter, turn on the light, and the room is full of friends and family shouting 'The party is over.' They are rehearsed and have a script. You are off-guard and dumbfounded.

George W. Bush has admitted having drinking problems in the past. From guarded newspaper revelations it seems that he was successfully 'intervened'. As best one can put it together, the 43rd President of the Union went on an epic bender in July 1986, culminating in his 40th birthday party. He had, one apprehends, been drinking heavily for at least ten years (he was 30 when he picked up the drunk-driving charge that threatened to scupper his presidential prospects, when it was divulged five days before the poll, in November 2000). Reportedly, his wife Laura had told him, 'maybe 50 times', that 'It's me or Jack Daniel's'. George chose Jack: 50 times. At the same time, 1986, Dubya's father George was Vice President and, one may assume, he did not want a son with a drink problem embarrassing *his* upcoming campaign for the White House. Barbara, like any mother, was worried about her wild boy.

The Bush parents arranged for their son to meet one-on-one with Billy Graham in 1986 at the family compound at Kennebunkport (this lends credence to the 'intervention' hypothesis). It was Billy's old-time religion – and the ultimatums of his family – that rescued young George from the demon drink. The free world may live to be grateful that the faith-based intervention worked. If it didn't work, we may not live to be grateful for anything. Would you want a dry-knuckle drunk (as Martin Sheen called Dubya) with his finger on the red button?

Ideally intervention, with its presentation of a Faustian choice to the drinker, needs to be done (as with George W.) when there is still much to lose, still people to care, and still a future career to live for. ('You can *still* be President, Son' – 'Naw! Do you think so, Dad?') Middle-class, 'respectable' drunks with caring families seem to respond best. The remedy seems to work most effectively with those who, like the Bush family, believe in 'faith-based cures' and the 'Jesus factor'.

All careers end badly, Enoch Powell famously declared, as his own went down the toilet. None more badly than that of the career-drinker. Even in a secular age, most of us would like to end well: like Addison, if we are really high-minded, who summoned young people to his death-bed, that they might witness the full dignity of a Christian's *quietus*.

Drunkards' deaths are awful; enough to drive you (and them) to drink. Worst of all are the deaths of drunken women. Their bodies are not made for hard drinking. Anthony Burgess, himself a problem drinker by his own account, dragged his wife down into a terrible alcoholic decline. He describes her last binge with self-mortifying, polysyllabic exactitude in the second volume of his autobiography, *You've Had Your Time*:

She had two more long sessions with me in pubs, both of which ended in violence, mine not hers... Back home Lynne complained of nausea. She tasted, she said, strong meat-extract in her throat. Then she turned pale, knowing what it was. A massive portal haemorrhage started while she lay in her bed: there were not enough pots and pans in the kitchen to hold the tides of blood... I read that alcoholic or portal cirrhosis was a chronic degeneration of the liver due to the prolonged ingestion of alcohol, characterised pathologically by increased interlobular fibrous tissue and degeneration of the liver cells, and clinically by obstruction to the portal circulation. The external symptoms Lynne had shown were revealed to be classic: tongue heavily furred; distended abdomen contrasting with wasting elsewhere; skin (the hepatic facies) dry, sallow, and icteroid: 'When ascites occurs, very bad: this is almost a terminal event.' One would need to be a St Julian to embrace that body, engage that breath. Ascites was the accumulation of serous fluid in the peritoneal cavity. The origin of the word was Greek *askos*, a wineskin. That was all too appropriate... I had always persuaded her to drink drink-for-drink with me, ignoring the truth that women's livers are not men's... It was right for me to feel like a murderer.

Zola, with his usual naturalistic unfeelingness, gives a vivid report of the female alcoholic's last infirmities in the description of poor Gervaise's degradation in *L'Assommoir*. As usual, the alcoholic woman is even more an object of moral contempt than her male partner:

Gervaise hung on like this for months, falling ever lower, swallowing the vilest insults, dying slowly of hunger, day after day. Whenever she got her hands on a few sous, she drank them up and pounded against the wall. Around the neighbourhood they gave her the dirtiest things to do. One evening they bet her she wouldn't eat filth. To earn the sous, she did eat it. Monsieur Marescot had decided to turn her out of the room on the seventh floor. However, as old Bru had just been found dead in his cubbyhole under the stairs, the landlord was willing to let her have this corner. Now she lived in what had been old Bru's niche. It was in that hole on a pile of old straw that she starved, with an empty stomach and chilled to the bone. Apparently, the earth did not want her. She became a maundering idiot, too dull to think of throwing herself from the seventh floor on to the courtyard pavement, and thus making an end of it. Death had to take her little by little, bit by bit, dragging out to the bitter end the damnable existence she had had. No one ever knew exactly what finally caused her death. They spoke of cold and of heat but the truth was that she died of poverty, of the accumulation of filth and weariness in her ruined life. According to the Lorilleuxs, she died like a pig in its sty. One morning, noticing a bad smell in the corridor, folks remembered that she had not been seen for two days. They found her in her cubbyhole already turning green.

Even Zola, for whom the human species was no more than a bacillus under the novelist's eyeglass, can scarcely bear to linger, it seems, and gives the description of Gervaise's last days in fast-forward mode.

Only some celestial audit could work out whether the fleeting happiness of inebriation is balanced by the terminal wretchedness of alcohol addiction. From the first glass of the blushful Hippocrene, with beaded bubbles winking at the brim, to the dog turd eaten for ten *sous* and the liver bursting like an over-distended plastic rubbish bag: how does it stack up? Good deal, bad deal? One would need a gigantic Benthamite pleasure–pain calculus: all those 'happy hours' in one pan; a seething mass of blood, broken bones, irritable bowels, foul breath and morning hangovers in the other.

For drinkers, the reckoning always nags. 'What are you

paying for this?' Most drunks could say, contemplating the glass in front of them, what Charlie Parker liked to quip about his glassine sachet of junk: 'There's my Steinway, my portfolio of stocks, my Cadillac.' Alcoholic remorse ('hangover') is universal. But one of the oddities of alcoholism is that few recovered alcoholics sincerely regret having suffered the disease (if disease is what it is). The Steinway, and portfolio are well lost; all for drink, as the dramatist might say.

This willingness to accept a manifestly bad bargain is one of the many paradoxes of alcoholism. It comes up at AA meetings frequently. Given their lives, most of the poor saps suffocating in tobacco smoke and sipping sour coffee out of dixie cups aver they would do it all again – but stop a bit sooner. Before, that is, the really bad things began (and, what is rarely admitted to, before the need for coming to these damn AA meetings and drinking this awful brew). There was, they nostalgically recall, a kind of adventure in it. A voyage to the end of one's night. At worst, alcoholism (for the 'recovering', at least) is a *felix culpa*: forbidden fruit worth eating, despite the curse (death, madness or, ultimate horror, lifelong sobriety!) that inevitably follows. Many drunks, even those surrounded with their life's wreckage, like to strike a Baudelairean pose: this *mal* has its *fleurs*.

And what, precisely, are they? Drunkenness, it is

protested, can be an educational experience – a spiritual or philosophical quest, even. It was only in the 'White Desert' of his alcoholic despair that Jack London was able to have his Schopenhauerian dialogues with what he calls in *John Barleycorn* the 'noseless one', Death. The Reaper would have disdained conversation with a sober interlocutor. Drunks cleave tenaciously to the illusion that drunkenness connects you with the inner truths of the universe, enables you to look God in the face. This is *vino*'s ultimate *veritas*.

Many can trip off a quatrain or two of *The Rubáiyát of Omar Khayyám*, that best known of Anacreontics, in support of the boozer's grand illusion:

> Come, fill the Cup, and in the Fire of Spring
> The Winter Garment of Repentance fling:
> The Bird of Time has but a little way
> To fly – and Lo! the Bird is on the Wing.

As they used to say of LSD, drink can be a trip. And if you don't take it, you'll never know.

Sometimes drunks can even persuade the sober world that their drunkenness is something grander than mere self-indulgence. When Charlie Parker's common-law wife asked the physicians to cure her gluttonously addictive husband – by the sledgehammer therapies of ECT or lobotomy, if necessary – she was asked: 'Mrs Parker what do you want? A husband or a genius?' A Strindberg spouse would have opted eagerly for mutilation; willing to apply the electro-pads to her man's forehead herself, if allowed to, if only for the pleasure of seeing the selfish bastard jump. Mrs Parker didn't, earning the eternal gratitude of jazz fans. She might have retorted, however, that a sober genius would have been welcome round the house at the kids' bedtime. 'Bird' died in his thirties (the surgeon who conducted the autopsy assumed the musician was in his sixties).

If not geniuses, most alcoholics feel special and believe that pathological drinking is a mark of their specialness. Like epilepsy in primitive societies, it is a kind of holy affliction. I suppose I, too, am grateful for alcohol – despite the wretchedness it brought me (and still does when I look back at all those years of waste and shame). It was, in its way, a solution.

I was, from childhood, afflicted with crippling 'shyness'; my light, for what it was, could never shine out from under the bushel of my social nervousness. It's easy (now) to see why I was awkward. I had been brought up an only child in wartime; there were no siblings; no role models; no dominant males against whom I could define myself. Thanks to German bombers, I went to seven schools before I was 11. And thanks to British bombers (in one of which my father was burned alive) I would never

37

enjoy the cosy stability of the postwar nuclear family. I was disadvantaged, but in no material way deprived ('pampered' and 'spoiled' were words I heard often when I displeased some elder; which, frankly, I did less often than most children). I wanted for nothing except normal boyhood society. My best relationships were with books. If Victor Frankenstein wanted to create an alcoholic in his laboratory, he could do worse than follow the preceding blueprint.

In adolescence, I needed some magic potion to help me connect with my male peers and – most urgently (given what was happening to my body) – with women. The romances of Rider Haggard and Dennis Wheatley (which I devoured from the ages of 11 to 13) no longer satisfied. I now wanted the real thing. Breaking the ice that kept the sexes apart was difficult in the 1950s; even for those possessed of style, good looks, quick wit, bravado and a winning line of 'chat'. I enjoyed none of those assets.

It would have been aeons before I took to the dance-floor sober (more so given the new 'steps' that were coming in: jive had given way to the 'creep'; Victor Sylvester's sedate rhythms were drowned out by Bill Haley's caterwaul; it was the end for the rituals of ballroom and ushered in frightening new anarchies). And never, had I waited till the end of time, would I have dared to place my hand on those forbidden zones of a young woman's body (well-guarded as they were in those days with brassieres that could have served as medieval armour and the impenetrably elastic 'roll-on'; I learned about lingerie hands-on, like other young males of my generation).

What emboldened me, and timorous youths like me, to the necessary pitch of sexual recklessness was gallons (literally) of bitter beer. Indulgence on this swinish scale did not make for urbane manners. The trick was to get the woman – who could be persuaded to drink 'shorts', as something more sophisticatedly feminine than 'pints' – even drunker, more 'incapable', than oneself (this, incidentally, was where the pre-alcoholic's tolerance sometimes came in handy). Acquiescent intercourse was the best that could be hoped for. Truly consensual sex in this pre-Pill era was something to be found only in the fantasies of Hank Janson, the leading pornographer of the day. What, one wondered, *was* a nymphomaniac? She was rarer than the unicorn in the Essex town of Colchester in the 1950s. Like other young men of the time, I was guilty, more than once, of what would now be called date rape. But never as often as I wanted, and never as often as those who were really good at it.

In their hearts, most drunks feel they were most truly alive in those days when they were most drunken. There is a husk-like dryness to the 'recovered' life, however fiercely joy in sobriety and pride in serenity are protested. Nor, having tasted the pleasures of excess, does moderation satisfy. Few alcoholics really want to return to 'social drinking' (a mistake that the medical profession often makes). Even now, with many years of sobriety behind him, Stephen King declares that social drinking 'would be like kissing my sister'. There is no juice or kick in it.

Raymond Chandler, a literary hall-of-fame alcoholic, eloquently describes the wasteland of post-alcoholic sobriety:

> The toughest thing about trying to cure an alcoholic or a user of dope is that you have absolutely nothing to offer him in the long run. He feels awful at the moment no doubt; he feels shamed and humiliated; he would like to be cured if it is not too painful, and sometimes even if it is, and it always is. In a purely physical sense, you maybe say he is cured when his withdrawal symptoms have passed, and they can be pretty awful. But we forget pain, and to a certain extent we forget humiliation. So your alcoholic cured or your former dope addict looks around him, and what has he achieved? A flat landscape through which there is no road more interesting than another. His reward is negative. He doesn't suffer physically, and he is not humiliated or shamed mentally. He is merely damned dull.

For men, excessive drinking, despite medical evidence that

it shrinks the penis and withers the scrotum, is intimately connected with the peacock displays of manhood. 'A man does not *exist* until he is drunk,' Hemingway declared. In his study *Hemingway vs Fitzgerald*, which depicts relations between the writers as a decades' long drinking match, Scott Donaldson records that the most shaming thing for Fitzgerald – the thoroughly bested contestant – was the fact that, compared to macho 'Papa', he drank 'like a girl'; when it came to booze, he was 'a cissy'.

On his part, Hemingway drank like a man – even inventing his own 'poison' for posterity to remember him by: the 'daiquiri'. (Michael Palin solemnly imbibes one of the syrupy concoctions, with the reverence of a communicant, in his popular pilgrimage book, *Hemingway's Adventure*.) Manly to the end, Hemingway died a madman, convinced, in the sodden wreckage of his alcohol-ruined mind, that the IRS and FBI were pursuing him for unpaid taxes. All those daiquiris down the hatch led to the shotgun barrel in the mouth at six o'clock in the morning in July 1961. (It was Hemingway's proud boast that 'he'd been drunk 1,547 times in his life but never in the morning'; he was clear-headed when he blew his head off.)

There is, as all adolescent drinkers know, something grand about excessive drinking. People tot up (and exaggerate) their tots because excessive drinking is, like sporting or athletic prowess, something that it is important to record. Norman Mailer, who has clearly veered into heavy drinking at 'Irish' periods of his career, notes as a matter of pride that he has done more damage to his brain with drink than by blows to the head sustained in his boxing days – which were also, of course, his drinking days.

This masculine-competitive drinking ethos ('drinking like a man') goes back to those old days in the wassail hall that we read about in *Beowulf*. After a day's slugging it out in the marsh with Grendel's mother, they would go back, sit on the 'yelping bench' in the wassail hall and get wasted on their filthy Anglo-Saxon ale, mead and wine. There is a particularly hilarious passage in the epic where, as the verse makes clear, a legless Beowulf – collapsed under his heroic intake of drink – is talking from the floor to a standing companion.

It was (and is) a warrior thing. The man who aspires to be a hero, wrote Samuel Johnson (an abstinent alcoholic in later life), must drink brandy: the 'infuriator'. The fact is that all drinking – if done to admirable excess – is heroic (I'm not entirely sure of Babycham). The illusion is timeless – look at *Ibiza Uncovered*, that fascinating TV-*verité* record of young British animals at play. It is a repetitive round of competitive drinking, competitive shagging and (off-camera) fighting. Imagine *Ibiza*

Undrunken or *Saudi Uncovered*, say. The imagination strains, and fails.

The long line of British 'hell-raisers' – from the Earl of Rochester to Oliver Reed – is a drunkards' line-up. Reed is an exemplary case. The years of his acting fame were decades of spree. Reed's preferred company was Beowulfian: club-rugby players, manual workers. His social life, in the high-earning years, was one of continuous, boisterous, glass-breaking knockabout: bawdy sing-song, press-up competitions, prick-measuring contests. He played *compère* and led the drunken charge. Reed relished the brutal camaraderie of the post-match piss-up in the public bar. He holds a kind of hell-raising record: 90 pints in three days, an orgy of swilling.

Oliver Reed died during the shooting of the movie of *Gladiator* (the film is dedicated to him). In Ridley Scott's screenplay he has the part of an old lion, a veteran of the arena, Proxime. On-screen, Reed's character suffers a nobly Roman death, holding his *rude* – the wooden sword that commemorated the manumission granted him by the emperor – as he is cut down by a pack of lesser swordsmen.

Off-screen, Reed toppled to his death off a bar stool in Malta, where *Gladiator* was being shot on location. It was the finale (*morituri te salutamas*) to a squalid session, during which he had drunk, it was reported, the equivalent of two bottles of Scotch. For all the awe and affection in which he was held, it is impossible not to regard Reed's career as one of wantonly wasted ability. His single talent was not buried, but drenched to extinction.

One knows, as a matter of course, precisely how much Reed consumed (wow!) on this last bender. Quantitative exactitude is an odd feature of excessive drinking. I do not think that spliff-puffers, or needle-toting addicts calibrate their overdoses as proudly as drinkers do their skinfuls. How many puffs did Clinton not inhale? How many grams of coke did Don Simpson (the Hollywood film producer) take on his last toot? Who's counting? They 'used'; that's all. How much is an 'OD'? How long is a piece of string?

Drinkers count neurotically (and not just volume; beer is, I think, the only intoxicant that can be consumed by the 'yard' from those peculiar tubular drinking vessels that one occasionally sees in traditional pubs). In his 1999 book *On Writing* (it's really about his drinking), Stephen King records that he knew he had a problem with alcohol when he calculated that he was 'drinking a case of 16oz tallboys a night'. A case is one up from a six-pack – 12 one-pint cans. With this regular nocturnal intake, King turned out a blockbuster, *Cujo*, 'that I barely remember writing at all'. It went straight to the top of the *New York Times*'s bestseller list; *that* he remembers.

One's glad that the author of *Cujo* (Dog from Hell) is now clean and sober and has the AA chips (13 years' worth) to prove it. But there is a kind of grisly one-up-manship about King's confession. This is a man who has written 30 books in 20 years, gets $40 million advances, and drinks a gallon-and-a-half a night *without even noticing*. You win, Steve. *Vicisti*, as Proxime would say.

Famously, Dylan Thomas ended his life on his knees before a young woman he had just met, with the ejaculation: 'I have just drunk 22 whiskies. I think that's the record. I love you.' He promptly died of what the autopsy called 'insult to the brain' (and compliment to the lady).

If Dylan had claimed a mere six Scotches, the scene would have fallen flat (although he might not have done). If William Hague had boasted of drinking a mere seven pints as a lad, he would still have been five times over the driving limit and well beyond the measly units permitted by the Portman Group (who presume to advise us about 'healthy' boozing while somewhat hypocritically being funded by those who produce booze). But 'one under the eight' would have seemed, you know, 'wimpish'. (Eight pints, or an imperial gallon, was the threshold of sobriety predicated by the British army in the old days, when soldiers were men and won wars rather than 'keeping the peace' like counsellors in khaki.)

Many drinkers, to their last gulp, remain convinced that they are in a contest that will confirm their manliness. They notch up their drinks with the morbid pride of gunfighters. (Are not empty bottles called 'dead men'?) Drinking lends itself to matches and tournaments. One is drinking for gold; chug-a-lugging for the Queen, my boys. It connects with that pervasive sense that drinking brings out one's full resources of manliness. Eugene O'Neill, who before topping himself drank a bottle of Scotch, left the other dead man there with the triumphant note: 'Never let it be said an O'Neill left a full bottle.' Beat that you bozos.

Alan Sillitoe's *Saturday Night and Sunday Morning* opens with a fine description of a drinking match. It is Saturday night (of course) in a Nottingham pub in the 1950s. Arthur Seaton, an uppity ('angry', that is) young man is enjoying to the full his youth in a postwar, morally liberated England. He can afford enjoyment on the high wages (with overtime as much as £15 a week) he is getting from the Raleigh cycle factory. Arthur is challenged by a 'loudmouthed' sailor to prove his manhood in the traditional, drunken way:

'What's the most you've ever drunk, then?' Loudmouth wanted to know. 'We used to have boozing matches on shore-leave,' he added with a wide, knowing smile to the aroused spectators. He reminded Arthur of a sergeant-major who once put him on a charge.

'I don't know,' Arthur told him. 'I can't count, you see.' 'Well,' Loudmouth rejoined, 'let's see how much you can drink now. Loser pays the bill.'

Arthur did not hesitate. Free booze was free booze. Anyway, he begrudged big talkers their unearned glory, and hoped to show him up and take him down to his right size. Loudmouth's tactics were skilful and sound, he had to admit that.

Having won the toss-up for choice, he led off on gins, and after the seventh gin he switched to beer, pints. Arthur enjoyed the gins, and relished the beer. It seemed an even contest for a long time, as if they would sit there swilling it back for ever, until Loudmouth suddenly went green half-way through the tenth pint and had to rush outside. He must have paid the bill downstairs, because he didn't come back. Arthur, as if nothing had happened, went back to his beer.

Arthur drinks three more pints. He then honks voluminously over some luckless customer in the pub before going back to give his current paramour (Brenda, a married lady) a good doing. It's a guy thing. Later in the novel, when Brenda gets royally squiffy on a bottle of warm gin, it's to procure the abortion of Arthur's love child – conceived in high drunkenness, of course.

Oddly, the cult of heroic drinking to toxic excess accompanies a frequent reluctance to speak plainly about the damage it patently does. Sillitoe nowhere suggests that the exuberant Arthur is pre-alcoholic (as any young fellow who drinks routinely 13 pints and seven gins of a Saturday night clearly is). There is a strange unwillingness to call drunks drunks and thus demystify the wonderful adventure of drinking. Take the following from Jon Stallworthy's (excellent) life of Louis MacNeice. The poet is approaching the end of his short and chronically confused life. He is on the brink of 'retiring' (ie, he has been discreetly let go) from the BBC – a sinecure which at least occupied some of his wakeful hours ('drinking time', that is). The South African novelist, John Cope, met the poet on the evening of 26 April 1961 in the foyer of Broadcasting House. It was time for the evening 'session'. MacNeice, of course, had primed the pump with a lunch-time session:

> MacNeice proposed a drink with friends, followed by a curry supper in an excellent place he knew. Hedli [one of MacNeice's troupe of lovers] was in the George but he avoided her, telling Cope he was worried that she might make a scene over 'another young woman' in his life. Drinks followed in quickfire succession. BBC people rolled in and out with the tide. Plans were made and unmade...

From the George they went by taxi to another pub and another and another. Cope kept reminding MacNeice of the promised curry supper. 'Yes – any minute,' he would unconvincingly reply. By the time they reached the Load of Hay on Haverstock Hill, Cope estimated he had drunk a dozen beers and MacNeice more than double that. It was close to closing time, and the Irishman (who was still steady on his feet, as the South African was not) ordered a row of drinks and a half-jack of whisky to tide him over the rest of the evening. He then went to the telephone 'to whistle up some girls'. but only managed to contact Nancy Spender, who must have heard the alcohol in his voice and declined to join them. When time was called, he emptied the last glass and, with his bottle, swayed out into the cold night.

A short walk brought them to a door at which MacNeice knocked. It was opened by his doctor, Jerry Slattery, and his wife Johnny, who took Cope into the kitchen and cut some sandwiches, which he ate gratefully. MacNeice looked at them, winced, finished his bottle of whisky, and fell asleep. The Slatterys told Cope this was a fairly common occurrence. MacNeice was almost living on alcohol and would sometimes go without food for days on end.

One may question whether the tally here is correct (any more than Thomas's '22 whiskies', which has been plausibly disputed by the poet's biographers). The human frame, particularly one as debilitated as MacNeice's, could surely not sustain something around 30 beers, and half a bottle of whisky, on top of a lunchtime intake and a chronically empty stomach.

None the less, MacNeice certainly drank a lot; a fatal dose, as it turned out. He died two years later, of what the biography euphemistically calls 'viral pneumonia', aged 56. He had, one assumes, pickled himself to extinction 20 years before his time. Alcohol killed him as indisputably as consumption killed Keats. But Stallworthy nowhere says that Louis MacNeice was an alcoholic – which he manifestly was. The biography delicately skirts the issue. MacNeice's life and talent, for all its wonderful creativeness, was – much of it – squandered; pissed away. Why not admit it?

Much the same might be said of Kingsley Amis. Huge offence was caused to the novelist's surviving family by Eric Jacobs's account of Amis's last days in hospital, sold for a huge (reportedly) amount of money, to the *Sunday Times*. Jacobs, a retired and evidently hard-drinking journalist, had formed his friendship with Amis over convivial lunches in the Garrick Club to which they both belonged. Jacobs visited his clubmate as he died, painfully, in hospital, and composed from his visits a picture of the novelist on his deathbed – a death surely accelerated by, if not directly attributable to, decades of very heavy drinking. Jacobs's eye-witness testimony represented a massive breach of good taste (and true friendship, one might think). But nowhere in his article or his earlier biography does Jacobs come out and say that Amis was alcoholic.

'Amis himself', Jacobs reports, always rejected the A-word 'as a term of abuse, not a diagnosis of clinical significance'. Amis's second wife, Elizabeth Jane Howard, was more forthright on the matter. At the time of the couple's separation, in 1980, 'she said she would return on certain conditions, the principal one being that Amis should give up drinking – not just moderate his intake or cut down a bit but stop completely and for ever. Drink, Jane argued, had been her husband's main problem, the chief reason why he had become unbearable and she could no longer live with him.'

As most adults can testify (given the universality of the disease) drunks die badly. Society none the less conspires with the alcoholic to suggest that the drunkard's death can be beautiful; an apotheosis. A notable example is the Oscar-winning film, *Leaving Las Vegas*. It narrates the last hours of an addicted boozer and gambler, played by Nicolas Cage. Having ruined himself at the tables, he is drinking himself to death ('the shortest way out of Las Vegas', as the grim old joke about Manchester and drink used to put it). The film ends, incredibly, with a

Liebestod. Despite having drunk himself to the lintel of death's door, the Cage character conquers his alcoholic impotence to have it off with a beautiful showgirl, who, in the few hours that they have known each other, surrenders to his fuddled glamour. His brewer's droop miraculously suspended, the Cage character rides out on the crest of the drunkard's priapic dream, a death fuck. He dies, erect, magnificent and prepotent. Dream on.

The hopeful myth that alcoholism does not diminish sexual attractiveness is (to take one of innumerable examples) reiterated in another recent film, *28 Days* (that being the period of time required for minimal detox in American sanitoriums). Sandra Bullock is shown in the early, pre-recovery phase of her story, disarrayed, falling-down drunk but eminently attractive (more so, one might think, for the moral recklessness of her incapable state; the appetitiveness of rattlesnakes comes to mind). Paul Newman – who must, I think, have an interest in problem drinking since he so often chooses alcoholic roles – is similarly unblemished by advanced alcoholism in *The Verdict* (or in any of his parts, going back through *Hud* to the closeted gay alcoholic Brick in *Cat on a Hot Tin Roof*). Regarded in its totality, the career of Newman is a defiant assertion that 'alcoholic stud' and 'alcoholic glamour' are not contradictions.

The assertion is raised to absurd heights in the biopic

of Charles Bukowski, *Barfly*. As played by Mickey Rourke (an off-screen 'hellraiser', of course), the cultish post-Beat writer is shown dissipating himself relentlessly. He is filthy. His breath could peel paint. None the less, he can fight like a champ, he can effortlessly seduce beautiful (sober) women. Above all, he can write like an angel. Take heart, drinkers of the world.

Not Drinking: Alcoholics Anonymous

Society is rarely keen on constructive measures to help alcoholics. Aid is expensive and grossly intrusive (alcoholism is, I think, the only non-infectious physical disease for which you can be 'sectioned' or locked away for the good of society). There are no votes in it as there are, say, in breast cancer, child leukaemia, or even − after Leah Betts − adolescent pill-popping. The condition is notoriously intractable and drunks are (as most think) a wholly lost cause by the time that medical intervention becomes an issue. Say 'cure' to an alcoholic and he will see in his mind's eye incarceration and the straitjacket, not the happy-ever-after of a sober life.

Society has an arsenal of blunt instruments used to keep drinking in check. Licensing was brought in − after some dramatic explosions − during the First World War to stop munitions workers (flush with all the overtime pay) drinking before and during work. In T.S. Eliot's 1922 poem, the call 'Drink up, please, it's *time*' was as topically new as 'I did *not* have sexual relations with that woman' is today. The law has been gradually relaxed, and licensing, after 80 years, is virtually a dead-letter in the UK. In metropolitan areas, the dedicated drinker can find a sales outlet at any hour of the day or night. There remain some vexatious anomalies (sometimes you have to buy a meal, or pay a membership fee to some fictional club; there are price hikes for drinking at anti-social hours). It may be a good thing. Informed opinion suggests that licensing actually exacerbates problem drinking, encouraging as it does 'bouts', 'binges' and 'Time, ladies and gentleman, *please*!' gulping.

Excise duty on drink is one of the oldest and most easily collected forms of taxation (it can be traced back to the Anglo-Saxon period). As a 'sin tax', it has the added attraction that it can be raised to astronomical levels (as it has been in Scandinavian countries) without effective protest. Indeed, this can be seen by the official mind as a form of taxation that is actually *good* for the taxpayer. Of course, it never works that way. It is astonishing what other comforts of life drinkers will do without to carry on drinking. Excise is the one source of income the Exchequer can always rely on: boom or slump. (I have always thought it significant that the Chancellor traditionally sips whisky and water while delivering his annual Budget statement.)

Prohibition in Western societies is nowadays imposed by age-qualification (the 'RU 16?' query in British pubs, 'carding' in American bars). Ever since the 'noble experiment' failed in America, total banning of drink – a 'war on alcohol' equivalent to the 'war on drugs' – has not been attempted in a Western society (there is a persuasive revisionist reading of American Prohibition, which argues that it did, for a short period, produce a healthier if unhappier population).

Over the last 30 years, savagely punitive strategies have been selectively applied, partly in response to pressure from such groups as MADD and moral panics about 'football hooligans'. Drunks are more likely, nowadays, to find themselves in prison (or walking to work). Paradoxically, there has been at the same time greater social tolerance for 'skid-row' destitution. Time was, 50 years ago, that street inebriates would be moved on or arrested as 'drunk and incapable'. Now, in most Western cities (unless there is some great public event, like the Olympic Games), they are permitted to lie in the gutters and doss in doorways unhindered.

Sex and drug education are a big deal in schools. But not alcohol education. Bizarrely, in Britain, serious instruction on 'sensible drinking' is outsourced to the suppliers of drink, through such bodies as the Portman Group (a lobby subsidised by the brewers and distillers; foxes and hen-coops come to mind).

In America, bottles and containers carry warnings (especially for pregnant women); but not in the UK. Education of the young – incorporating practical experiments in the classroom – might well be a very effective way of training the young to handle a risky product, advertising for which will bombard them every day of their adult lives. But no political party is going to risk electoral suicide by advocating seminars on controlled boozing in schools. The unofficial drinking schools that form in university union bars are notoriously reckless: nurseries for alcoholism ten years down the road.

The cures which the medical profession has devised for alcoholism have their vogue, only to be replaced with more voguish successors. All seem to say more about the period in which they originate than the nature of the condition. What they have in common is a general tendency not to work. The one remedy which does (perhaps) work is Alcoholics Anonymous.

AA was the invention of two men. Robert Smith ('Dr Bob'), a proctologist, stolid by nature, and a heavy drinker (at least, given his specialism, he never had to breathe on his patients), had, despite his habit, contrived to hold down his professional job and family in the middle-sized mid-American town of Akron, Ohio. In 1935, when he touched bottom, the other man, William Wilson ('Bill W.') was a failed stockbroker and a fully-fledged dipsomaniac. At a Faustian moment in Akron's Mayflower Hotel – poised between the bar and the telephone – Wilson had the happy thought that talking to another drunk might stave off another disastrous session. One thing led to another: clandestine meetings, the invention of the 'anonymity' gimmick, the *Big Book*, '12 steps', '12 traditions', worldwide expansion.

AA had some obviously historical precursors (notably the Washington Temperance Society). And one can speculate plausibly about supra-personal, socio-historical forces that combined to form AA at this particular period: the Roaring Twenties, Prohibition, the 1929 crash (which ended Wilson's good times), and the 1930s cult of heroic drinking (which led to AA's cult of heroic abstention), celebrated in the work of such contemporaries as Scott Fitzgerald and Ernest Hemingway.

From the apostolic few who gathered in the basement of King School in Akron, Ohio, in June 1935, Alcoholics Anonymous has grown into the largest secular self-help organisation for sick people in the Western world. It's bigger than the Masons, Oxfam, the Rotarians, the Elks, the Trades Union Congress, the White Aryan Resistance, the Samaritans, Ku-Klux Klan, the Women's Institute, and – in terms of dutiful weekly attendance – the Church of England.

AA is big. So is alcoholism. But the fellowship's corporate grandeur rests on mysterious foundations. Given the inviolable 'tradition' of anonymity ('the spiritual foundation of all our traditions, ever reminding us to place principles before personalities'), no one actually knows how effective the 'Program' is therapeutically. Estimates vary from the 75 per cent success-rate claimed in the fellowship's more optimistic promotional material to the bleak word-of-mouth wisdom (current in LA meetings) that 'only one in 30 makes it to a six-month chip'.

There is some evidence for the pessimistic view. 'Old-timers', as they are affectionately called, observe that in most groups newcomers outnumber them. If, as they like to say, 'It works!', the population of the long-term sober in AA should grow year by year into a majority. It doesn't. Is it because members graduate from the fellowship into truant sobriety? Or, horrible thought, do most of those who pass through the meetings 'lapse'?

AA, one concludes, is either the only nationwide, affordable alcoholism treatment that truly works, or it is a gigantic con: the drinker's grandest illusion. No one knows for sure. My own view (based on two decades of intermittent attendance in the US and the UK) is that AA rescues three kinds of alcoholic. 'Low-bottom' drunks who have lost everything else can creep into the fellowship and live an institutionalised existence. Like Poor Tom's hovel, AA is their shelter from the storm of the real world.

The second kind to derive help from AA is the 'high-bottom' alcoholic on the brink. Someone, that is, who still has a job, a family, a place in society – but who is in imminent risk of drinking all that away. For such drunks (I was one of them), AA supplies a breathing space and a springboard back to a sober, or at least more controlled, way of life.

The third, and most interesting of those who thrive in AA are the virtuosos of the fellowship: mystics of sobriety and gurus of recovery. My guess is that the majority of those who come to meetings eventually go out to continue their drinking careers as unsaved by AA as by all the other remedies: atropine aversion therapy, antabuse, ECT, acupuncture, snake-pits – and, doubtless, in a year or two, gene-replacement therapy.

Authorities in the US take a very upbeat view of AA; it is, after all, as American as its airline namesake. The Program is integrated into court-sentencing practice in many states. Convicted DUIs (intoxicated drivers) are routinely obliged, in addition to other humiliations (handcuffing, a night in the drunk tank), to attend a course of AA or NA (Narcotics Anonymous). Typically, this means attendance at a dozen meetings.

In large conurbations these pressed men can nowadays make up a sizable part of the AA congregation. They tend to be a surly crew; not least because they have had to come to the meeting by public transport. Baffled by the proceedings and frequently pissed in both the American and British sense of the term, they can't wait to get their court cards signed and reclaim their driving privileges.

Whether attendance is conceived by American judges as condign punishment (like Volpone being confined with the *incurabili*), as rehabilitation, or as moral tagging is unclear. It's likely the courts do it as a sop to the immensely powerful pressure-group, MADD (who would really rather drunk-drivers were strung up on piano wire). Court-coerced drunks benefit little from AA – but they give the organisation a valued seal of official approval.

AA has similarly come to serve as an approved outpatient facility for the American health industry. Medical-benefit policies are specific about what treatment they will provide for addiction – typically a chronic and intractable condition. Coverage tends, in most plans, to be limited to a month per year, per family member.

Residential care for alcoholics – in what used to be called sanatoriums – is costly: the cheapest institutions run at around $5,000 a week; the most fashionable (such as the Betty Ford Clinic, at the delightfully named Rancho Mirage) cost much more.

The health management organisations (HMOs), which were set up in the US in the 1980s specifically to keep medical costs under control, take a dim view of alcohol rehabilitation. If you are hospitalised for a drinking problem in the US what routinely happens is a crash-course of 'detox and counselling' after which (within a few weeks at most) the still trembling patient is released into AA on a fire-and-forget basis. The prospect for these unfortunates is poor.

In its totality, AA resembles nothing so much as a terrorist network. There is no central organisation as such – just a honeycomb of cells on the ground, none of which directly communicate with each other, with HQ, or with the outside world. The Tenth Tradition is fundamental to the operation of these bodies: 'AA has no opinion on outside issues; hence the AA name ought never be drawn into public controversy.' The fellowship has no views on politics or on anything (even alcoholism). It is pure praxis. On the ideological level, it remains faithful to its founder Dr Bob's dying injunction to the faithful: 'Keep it simple.' Empty, that is, of complicating doctrine or confusing theory.

Nothing is emptier than the AA purse. The organisation accumulates no cash, capital or material assets.

There are good reasons for this austerity. Alcoholics (whether practising or recovering) are hopeless with money. As well give them whisky. Those groups which collect funds to set up their own premises or accumulate treasuries for good works inevitably collapse in a welter of recrimination and relapse.

AA survives by virtue of its peculiar brand of communism. There are no dues. It will not accept bequests. Meetings are self-supporting (usually with a dollar in the basket – the Seventh Tradition). Any money surplus to immediate requirements (typically the hire of a dusty church hall, an urnful of acrid coffee and some cookies) is given away before it can do any harm.

The ritual of the AA meeting is familiar even to lifelong teetotallers from (usually melodramatic) depictions on film and TV. The alcoholic enters the meeting denuded of his or her identity, with only a forename between them and the similarly nameless group. The speaker 'qualifies' by confession: 'My name is [Nicholas or Mary] and I am an alcoholic.' If the speaker is a newcomer, a hearty round of applause will follow this bald proclamation. After that, beans are spilled. It is not merely identity which is blanked out by the anonymity gimmick – but social rank and hierarchical status. It is conceivable that a judge and the criminal he has sentenced can meet in a meeting. I once, to our mutual embarrassment, came face to face with a junior colleague.

There are two main varieties of AA meeting: 'Speaker' and 'Participation'. As the names suggest, in one you will listen, in the other you may talk. The discourse in the Participation groups is distinctive. Dialogue (in AA-speak, 'cross-talk') is proscribed. One does not address one's fellow-alcoholics, one 'shares'. It looks to the outsider like seminar discussion but isn't. It's a bunch of people musing aloud; a kind of self-willed collective autism; pure Samuel Beckett. The ban on cross-talk is, like much else in AA's procedure, prophylactic. Bad things happen when alcoholics communicate too directly with each other, as any bartender knows. Tempers are lost, fists are raised, nails brandished, knives and guns come out.

The disciplines and practices of AA are paradoxical in the highest degree – but no crazier than drinking, as its members never tire of pointing out. Warmth is over-powering within the group. But outside the group members shun each other's company. There are no Masonic handshakes or codewords. This, too, is motivated by prudence.

Alcoholics are typically dysfunctional individuals – particularly with each other. The first informal advice newcomers tend to be given is: (1) never borrow money or lend it to a fellow alcoholic; (2) never buy a car from a fellow alcoholic; (3) above all, never fuck a fellow alcoholic. Outside the cloying intimacy of the group, it is a fellowship of strangers.

An exception is made for the 'sponsoring' relationship – something universally encouraged but not formalised by the Program. Newcomers are always told to immerse themselves in AA – 90 meetings in 90 days is the standard prescription. At its simplest, this is a weaning process; something to fill the huge socket left in the former drinker's life where booze used to be. It is also, as any psychologist will recognise, standard induction routine – especially when associated with physical exhaustion (few detoxing drunks sleep well). But, however many meetings he dutifully attends, the newcomer will probably need day-round support: a babysitter, that is, to call when a 'slip' is imminent – perhaps at some grossly anti-social hour of the night. This is where the sponsor comes in.

Necessarily, the sponsor–sponsee relationship flouts the non-hierarchical conventions, the prohibition on cross-talk and the anonymity principle. It can lead to emotional dependency and exploitation. There are suggested safeguards. Cross-gender sponsorship is strongly discouraged. Ideally, the sponsor should be the elder of the pair (in years and sobriety) – allowing a mellowly avuncular relationship to develop. But sponsoring is fraught with difficulty and is a component of the AA machine that often goes wrong. It is abuse of the sponsoring relationship that led, most recently, to accusations that AA is a cult – scientology for drunks.

Bill W. and Dr Bob's organisation is, of course, much nobler than L. Ron Hubbard's bunco scheme. AA meetings are, with baseball games, the only truly democratic events in America. The typical AA group is an *omnium gatherum* in which all sectors of American life and society are represented in conditions of genuine social equality. Alcoholism is no respecter of class.

Clustered around the big meetings are myriad self-selecting grouplets (usually Participation meetings) of a more homogeneous kind: tinkers, tailors, soldiers, sailors, rich men, poor men, beggar-men, thieves all have their own AA sessions. These tend to be closed occasions, unadvertised in the fellowship's 'blue book' or websites. They can be hard to find unless you doubly 'qualify'. Many Hollywood stars, for example, attend AA. But you won't find yourself sitting next to Christian Slater – unless you happen to be in the industry and making seven-figure alimony payments. There is no copyright on the 12-step Program and any number of imitative therapies have borrowed it: Al-Anon, Al-Ateen, Chocanon, MA (Marijuana Anonymous), Weightwatchers. Most are pallid imitations.

AA's theology and medical science are primitive but serviceable. The movement was largely inspired by Frank

Buchman's Oxford Movement (the same movement that gave us Moral Rearmament and Mrs Whitehouse). True to its enthusiastic origins, AA believes in the regenerating effect of 'total' confession of sin and human inadequacy: 'We admitted we were powerless over alcohol [but] came to believe that a Power greater than ourselves could restore us to sanity' (in the original 1939 formulation, the salvationary word was 'God', not 'Power'). Evangelical Christianity remains the dominant flavour in AA's ideological mix. There are few more culturally perplexing sights than seeing a group in, say Beverly Hills, composed largely of alcoholic Jews having to finish a meeting with a choric recitation of the Lord's Prayer.

The 'higher power' to which AA members are obliged to surrender themselves as their second step to sobriety is manifestly the deity of Billy Graham, Lord Longford and Jeanette Winterson's mother. AA has always been an aggressively evangelical movement. The twelfth and final step – that of carrying the AA message to the 'alcoholic who still suffers' – imposes the role of proselyte on every active member of the fellowship (if I were conscientious, I would insert a website address here).

Medically, AA cleaves to the disease concept of alcoholism. Those 'alcoholics who still suffer' are conceived to be in the grip of an illness that is 'cunning, baffling and powerful'. The recovering alcoholic is never cured – but must imagine himself in a kind of protracted remission; as with the diabetic, relapse is always imminent (particularly if you stop going to meetings – the insulin analogy is often made). AA holds to the superstition that the alcoholism progresses inexorably, even when you are not drinking. Should you fall off the wagon, after 20 years of sobriety, your disease will be two decades more terminal. 'Rust', as Neil Young (the alcoholic's favourite balladeer) puts it, 'never sleeps.'

The belief that they are victims of an illness allows recovering alcoholics to forgive themselves for the awful things done in drink. Few alcoholics, by the end of their drinking careers, have not committed offences that the sober mind shudders at. But, although AA subscribes to the disease of alcoholism, it despises the medical establishment whose business disease is. Routinely at meetings, scorn is poured on the 'ignorant professionals'. As a favourite joke puts it: 'There are those who say doctors don't know everything. And there are those who say doctors don't know nothing.' AA is firmly of the second party.

Alcoholics have good reason for disliking doctors and psychiatrists and for jeering at their ignorance (despite the fact that doctors themselves are notoriously prone to alcoholism). Traditionally, the medical schools and teaching hospitals of America and Europe have given their students abysmally inadequate instruction on the nature of the ailment.

Many alcoholics who apply for treatment find the conventional health services too busy to mollycoddle sots like them. There are patients with real illnesses to treat: broken bones, cancer and acne. Sitting two hours after appointment time in the waiting room at the Maudsley hospital in south London (Bedlam, as it once was), with a splitting hangover, in the company of the stark staring mad is a foretaste of hell. AA bases its good works on the shrewd analysis that drunks know better how to deal with fellow drunks than doctors for whom drunks are a job of work or raw material for a career-advancing research project. AA places special stress on welcoming rituals, designed to allay the newcomer's crippling shame and make him feel at home. And genuinely wanted.

The trickiest aspect of the AA Program is its moral prescriptions. While accepting that the alcoholic is sick, AA enjoins them none the less to 'make direct amends' for past misdeeds committed under the influence. From a purely practical point of view this Ninth Step is a vital part of the Program. It requires the penitent husband and father, for example, to go back to his injured family, to square things with his cheated partner, and settle up with his creditors as best he can. 'Cleaning house' is the homely metaphor AA applies to this phase of recovery.

AA, originating as it did in small-town America, is strenuously opposed to what it scornfully calls 'geographical' cures: that is, making a new start in a new place. You get sober where you got drunk.

The 'amends business' is, however, deeply contradictory. The alcoholic is reassured he is the victim of disease – no more responsible for his misdeeds than a tubercular is for coughing. Yet, at the same time, he should regard himself as a repentant sinner who must fully atone for what he has done. Recovery, as AA defines it, requires energetic doublethink to be brought to a successful conclusion.

The architecture of the AA meeting is a mixture of the rigid and the fluid. Speaker meetings are organised around a liturgy of quite stunning tedium: readings from the *Big Book*, prayers, the award of monthly chips and anniversary cakes (accompanied by toe-curling choruses of 'Happy Birthday'), hand-holding, embracing, chants ('Hi, John!'). This is evidently necessary to create a structure for the incoming drunk in freefall or those whose sobriety is fragile. The structure is always there and always the boring same; a reassuringly solid thing in a dangerously liquid world.

What is rarely boring is the drunkard's tale, which every Speaker meeting features. It occupies the central position of the sermon in a conventional church service.

'Our stories', as the AA dogma puts it, 'disclose in a general way what we used to be like, what happened, and what we are now.' Every drunk has a story in him. AA wants to hear it. Speakers are applauded for their skill and humour in telling their stories (homily and gravity is disliked; a little pathos is OK). For large meetings, the invitation to speak is honorific and the best speakers build up a faithful following.

Participation meetings follow the Quaker pattern. They tend to be patronised by alcoholics well beyond the tremulous 90-day threshold; initiates who have learned how to talk the talk. They talk as the spirit moves. Often an abstract theme will be proposed: 'Faith', 'Hope' or 'Charity', for example. But the subsequent 'sharing' quickly becomes a freewheeling affair; anecdotes, not stories, predominate. The dynamics of both kinds of meeting put a premium on eloquence and theatrical display of ego. The dominant rhetoric is a kind of Twainian vernacular. At American AA meetings you will find descendants of ring-tailed roarers, pork-barrel philosophers, stand-up comedy of a high order, wit, and a broad vein of red-neck shrewdness. It can be very entertaining. As much fun as drinking, as they like to say, but without the hangover and all for a dollar.

Can AA survive? It has outlasted the death of its founders (Dr Bob went in 1950, Bill W. in 1971). But the fellowship's apparatus is clearly in need of some doctrinal overhaul – something that its lack of central organisation, or living patriarchs, renders tricky. The *Big Book*, the fount of AA wisdom, is – after 60 years and some ten million sales – creakingly anachronistic. A glaring example is the crucial Fourth Step, which obliges alcoholics to make 'a searching and fearless moral inventory of ourselves'.

'Making moral inventory' is a figure of speech which would have made perfect sense to a 1930s white-collar clerical worker – a Dagwood Bumstead or a Babbitt – familiar with small-store stock-control. It would make sense to a grocer's daughter from Grantham ('Our name is Margaret, and we are not an alcoholic'). The notion of 'making inventory' makes less sense to multi-addicted Hispanic kids from the barrio for whom small stores are something you break into.

What is most valuable in AA and should not be lost is the set of pragmatic tools which it has evolved over the years; its working parts. It remains, as a no-cost and (probably) effective treatment for an insolubly epidemic problem, the brightest of America's thousand points of light. But the movement desperately needs a New Testament and a Messiah for the new millennium, 'Jesus C', where are you?

My Story

Like *The Thousand and One Nights*, AA is an organisation founded on never-ending narrative. You recover
by telling your story, and hearing the stories of fellow
alcoholics. It is not a 'talking' but a 'tale-telling' cure.
The alcoholic's tale is distinctively different from other
verbal therapies: the Catholic's confession, the Puritan's
cleansing 'spiritual autobiography', or the Freudian
analysand's grudging revelations on the solitary couch.

The AA story has a distinct poetics. It is, in essence, a
narrative of inexorable loss, sudden epiphany and gradual
recovery. Typically, it starts with a well-ordered life,
progressively disordered by drink. At the critical moment
– it is conventionally a brief and irrecoverable interval –
the drunkard 'touches bottom'; he/she experiences their
fleeting 'moment of clarity'. Ideally, this is the moment
of introduction to AA. One comes in. Thereafter, if it
has a happy ending, the story becomes one of successful
(and never-ending) struggle. 'Recovering'. One never again
goes out.

AA is unusual in being a therapeutic organisation built
on ritualised oral storytelling to an initiated audience.
They do it very well (as Sylvia Plath said of her own
desperate remedy, suicide). Telling tales (most of them

72

tall, many of them self-serving) is one of the few things that booze makes you good at. Drunks are practised fictioneers; they live the creative lie and use a tissue of fibs to hold their rickety lives together. Drunks become fluent over the years at coming up with cover stories for such ticklish questions as: 'Just *how* much did you have to drink last night?... *Where* were you until four in the morning?... *How* did that scrape get on the car?... Is that *lipstick* on your collar?'

Two things have dominated my adult life: booze and prose fiction. I have been lucky to live in a time when both are in ample supply. With a PhD on the English novel, a fiction reviewer's slot on various London papers, and an alcoholic's insatiable thirst, I was multiply qualified for entry to AA – when I finally got round to it.

One of the things that first attracted me into the fellowship was its stories. For someone like me it was as magnetic as a campfire in the woods at night. One of the reasons I stopped going to meetings regularly was that, in the last analysis, I didn't really have a good enough story myself. I couldn't match, let alone top, the tales I heard at AA. Not, that is, if I were 'uncompromisingly honest', as the Program requires. In my heart, I knew I had never been a truly heroic drinker. Nor was I, in sobriety, an epic storyteller. But being in the company of those who were was, while it lasted, a thrill. When, nowadays, I go to meetings it is often to hear someone I particularly admire – as, for example, I admire and seek out the latest novels of John Updike, or Muriel Spark, or Martin Amis.

This, however, is to advance things. I touched bottom, as alcoholics like to say, on 12 February 1983 (the date is slightly fuzzy). I had just taken up a position as professor of literature at the California Institute of Technology. Caltech, as it is popularly known, is a small, excessively well-endowed science institution in Pasadena. Pasadena itself is a small, genteel western town, seven minutes away, by freeway, from downtown Los Angeles. LA is neither small nor genteel.

The Caltech job was, in career terms, one of those lucky breaks of which you can normally expect two or three in a professional lifetime. Playing such opportunities right is the big challenge of the academic career. It's not easy. You generally have two options: you can move, or you can use the 'offer' as leverage to feather your present nest. Or you can play games – moving from counter-offer to counter-offer or taking yourself, as a 'property', to a third potential employer.

The right call is rarely easy. In the early 1980s there were, however, circumstantial factors pushing me away from my home country; what in chess is called a forced move. The decade had ushered in a dark age for seats of British learning – the darkest since the dissolution of the monasteries, as we muttered in our gloomy common rooms. Keith Joseph's punitive regime of 'cut and freeze' had just taken hold. The Tories had hated the university sector ever since turbulent students (reds, all of them) pelted their party's MPs with eggs and obscenities at campuses in the 1960s. Oxford's refusal of an honorary degree for Mrs Thatcher in 1985 and 1987 sealed their enmity.

This was payback time. In the name of 'efficiency' (as if this abstract commodity was what universities produced, not research and education) the DES, as it was then called, embarked on a purge of Stalinist ferocity. A whole generation of middlingly senior academics was sent into what was euphemistically called 'early retirement' in the name of 'systems re-engineering' in the higher education sector. Colleagues were decanted by the dozen into their premature sunset years. You could hardly teach for the sound of falling timber ('dead wood' as the authorities liked to call it, as they lustily hacked away at the tree of British higher learning).

I was 45 – mid-life-crisis years. I was a decade too young for the chop. My wood was still sappy enough. But neither was I young or flexible enough to ride the changes with the sense of infinite growing time ahead. I did not, as George Eliot puts it, have my '35 years ahead of me'.

There is a shadow-line in working life: the point at

which you understand pensions. I was just beginning to penetrate the mysteries of the Universities' Superannuation Scheme: about halfway, that is, through the panels of that old Pearl Insurance cartoon advertisement ('They tell me the job doesn't have a pension. Ho hum'). And, of course, I was also halfway through my career (40 years, as the USS actuaries calculate it). The Dantean juncture. At this point one begins to hunger for spoils, signs of success: promotion, honorific titles, high salary, 'Top of the world, Ma!' recognition of one's life achievements. These awards were in short supply in British universities in the early 1980s. 'Holding on' was the priority. Forget slippery poles. Standing up to one's neck in the slough of British higher education, America glowed like the city on the hill.

The Caltech offer came through a grandee in my subject, J. J. ('Jerry') McGann. Jerry had himself just been appointed to head the literature group at Caltech. Teaching humanities at this exclusively scientific institution was, as colleagues ruefully observed, something of a fifth wheel on the buggy. There were, most years, no majors in literature and few graduates in any humanities subject. But, in compensation, Caltech paid humanists on the same level as scientists, and they gave their scientists what big-brains like them could expect in the commercial sector. This, they had decided, was the only way to get the best. The institute was loaded, could afford to pay top whack, and its governors were generous by nature. Caltech was a science gravy-train, but one on which humanists could hitch a ride. In short, they offered me $50,000 – three times my UK salary (add to that Caltech's faculty housing plan and the difference was out of sight).

McGann was the best in his field and Caltech had gone over the odds (magnitudes more than my measly 50 grand) to lure him from Johns Hopkins and all the other universities that were throwing offers at him. He was, as they liked to say, 'hot'. More importantly, McGann was reshaping his discipline, working on new lines in 'material bibliography', redefining the literary object in interesting new ways. He has an indefatigably lively mind. And he was, everyone who worked with him confirmed, a good colleague: high flyer and nice guy. The salary which Caltech came through with in 1982, with benefits, was plausibly rumoured to be the highest for a professor of English in the US. This prize has since probably passed to Stanley Fish at Illinois. We are, of course, talking sums not far off a quarter of a million dollars. I go into this fiscal detail to stress that America was (and is) in a different league from Britain. And Caltech heads that league. It can afford to fetter its faculty with golden chains.

McGann was by nature expansionist. He wanted to

build his group, and it was my good luck that he liked my work. In his eyes, I was, if not 'hot', attractively warm. My line at that time was the relatively new sub-discipline of publishing history, or 'book trade studies'. It fit nicely with McGann's then interests. Caltech's offer to me in the first instance was a one-year 'visiting' appointment. It would enable us to look each other over. If we liked what we saw, it was on. One could see it as a kind of trial marriage.

My other marriage was meanwhile going to hell. My drinking had been dangerously excessive for some years. It was now spinning out of control – though usually in the form of out-of-hours, weekend or vacation binges (what, for normal married men, would be 'time with the family'). At my loved ones' bruised insistence (blackmail!) I had been seen at the Maudsley, armed with a letter of introduction from a senior physician friend (I was no common-or-garden drunk, for god's sake). The letter cut no ice.

After a brief consultation with the registrar (a famous name in British alcohol studies, who was then touting a 'controlled drinking' field experiment), I was referred to one of his juniors. He turned out to be the nicest psychiatrist I have ever met. But his prescription was drastic. I must give up drinking altogether, he ordained. A fortnightly one-on-one meeting (which meant hours in the ghoulish waiting room for 40 minutes' counselling) would keep me to this regime. The theory was that, if I could stay off the booze for 18 months, the 'prognosis' was good for permanent recovery. This was what the unit's research was currently telling them. Perhaps they were right. I never made it to the finishing line.

I manfully went on a year's white-knuckle 'dry drunk', as AA jargon puts it. This was 1980. It didn't last. The nice psychiatrist moved on (the good ones always do; like academics, they get 'offers'). He was replaced by a doctor who, however knowledgeable, seemed much more neurot-ic than I was. And he manifestly didn't like me. I felt like a specimen. A cockroach and entomologist relationship, as it seemed to me. Gregor Samsa and his shrink.

My dry spell did not last. It corroded gradually, like an old dam giving way under the pressure of that vast lake of booze on the other side. I would manage six weeks (a painfully long period, for an abstaining alcoholic) before jumping out of the groove – usually for an explosively brief bout, but long enough to smash things up. Remorse would get me back on the wagon – but for a shorter period than the last. By January 1983, when I went off to California, I was on the terrible merry-go-round of what AA calls 'periodics'. I would be sober for weeks, sodden-drunk for days, bitterly remorseful for hours, and sober again. So the wheel turned. This is a peculiarly destructive phase of drinking, physically, and socially. Having lapsed, one drinks to madly toxic levels – making up for lost time, suffused with guilt and apprehensive of the dry, remorseful weeks to come before the next glorious release. The gross drunkenness shatters the trust others put in you. Usually after the third or fourth such lapse they give up on you. I was well past that threshold. The carousel was speeding up, like the climax of *Strangers on a Train*.

Professionally, I would still be classified as a 'high functioning' alcoholic. I could do my job. There were occasional disasters: drunkenly slurred lectures (*à la* Lucky Jim), student complaints about late return of essays (*à la* Butley), missed meetings, insulted colleagues, dinner-party disasters (some of which can still make me groan out loud today). But I could just about cope at work. I was experienced enough, after 20 years, to fly on automatic pilot, winging it, as they say. It helped greatly that in academic life you largely devise your own schedule. Cannily (as I thought – alcoholics love to think of themselves as smart operators), I ensured that the bulk of my lectures, tutorials and seminars were in the hung-over but clear-headed morning – before the dangerous fog of the lunch session descended on the world. If I had something important to write (a piece for the *London Review of Books*, say), I could stay sober.

My head of department at UCL, Karl Miller (he was also, fortuitously, editor of the *LRB*), came from journalism (and, further back, from Scotland). He knew all about drunks and was infinitely patient. Domestically, it was something else. One of the problems about problem drinking is that you tend to be at your drunkest and least civilised at night – when, that is, you go home. If your family is still around, 'scenes' are inevitable. Few women nowadays wield the cartoonist's rolling-pin, or throw crockery at their drunken spouse's head. But their long-brewed disapproval scalds the alcoholic (who will already be feeling remorse, probably) like molten lead. By the time you get back, the little woman has her script rehearsed to perfection.

What defence do you have? None. Guilt makes the drunk quarrelsome and few alcoholics – when drunk and quarrelsome – are not violent, verbally and physically. Anger is, late in the game, exacerbated by sexual paranoia (the alcoholic's impotence translates into jealousy of Othello-like intensity). And, of course, there is the sheer nastiness of the Edward Hyde everyone has inside them. Edward thrives on booze.

On at least one occasion, I had been physically abusive to my wife and son. Drunks do these things (and worse). The horror of having done them makes it harder to sober up, paradoxically, so one does them again and again: if the victims hang around. After a while every drunk drinks to forget what he has done (and will again do) when drunk. Anger is one deadly sin the drunk is prone to. Gluttony, of course. Jealousy, yes. And, of course, lechery. I had, for some years, been having extramarital affairs.

Another significant detail of the drunk's timetable is that he (in my case) tends to be at his best at lunchtime. Flirting time, that is. At lunch the drunk, still not entirely tanked up, is lively, bonhomous, and well this side of stupefaction. Academic life has lots of convenient holes in the day, which one can use for alternative lives. Few university teachers have more than 20 contact hours a week. And London is the ideal city for running multiple lives and for clandestine relationships. One lies to every-one, of course, to keep things in place. And what the alcoholic wants, most of all, is to keep his ducks in line so that he can drink. That is always the bottom line. Sexual delinquency is a symptom, not the goal.

Keeping the Sutherland show on the road was not easy. My wife every so often walked out with our young son. She was, after 15 years with me, something of a co-alcoholic, an 'enabler' (as the AA lexicon puts it). But she had her pride and her breaking-point. She had, I knew, seen a solicitor – and, as I suspected (in my alcoholic's paranoia), possibly someone unprofessionally as well. I don't now think that she had. But who could have blamed her?

It was a mess. Alcohol didn't make things simpler, but

it blurred them temporarily into invisibility. Leaving the country for a new start in southern California was a heaven-sent 'geographical' cure. More so since the Caltech offer was so munificent and, thanks to the tax amnesty, all net income. I could be ostentatiously generous – something that drunks love to be (it allays their sense of guilt at drinking up the housekeeping money for all those years). I could, assuming I could find time and energy to live them, afford several lives.

Caltech was easy street. Teaching was minimal (six hours a week, 20 weeks a year, small classes); the students were clever, well-mannered and intellectually docile (all they really wanted was to preserve their perfect 4.0 GPA – grade-point average). And there were no administrative chores. Who knew, I might even get round to doing some research at the nearby Huntington Library ('If I died and went to heaven,' a colleague once told me, 'it would be like having an eternity-fellowship at the Huntington'). If all else failed, there was always Disneyland.

I left the UK in high spirits arriving in the US for New Year. My wife, working with a prestige London publisher, was not inclined to accompany me. The bonds holding us together were frayed to breaking-point. If it was a trial marriage with Caltech, it was a trial divorce with her. There was an unspoken agreement that if I cleaned up things might mend. But, for the moment, I was free as air.

I got a small apartment near campus, ingratiated myself by day – and promptly disgraced myself at night by getting drunk and boorish at various welcoming functions. It wasn't misjudgment: more like taking deliberate aim and shooting yourself in the foot.

It is a peculiarity of alcoholics that, when things go well, they sabotage themselves. This death wish is often pondered at AA meetings. My personal view is that drunks do not want the responsibility of a successful life. It involves too many decisions and too much stress. 'Keep it simple' is truly the drunk's motto. Nothing simpler than disaster. Smash the crockery and you never have to wash it up.

Another favourite explanation is that by misbehaving drunks are confirming to themselves that, however extreme their misbehaviour, someone will always be there to look after them. They want to regress to that childhood condition where they can soil their nappy and still be loved ('Who's a bad boy, then?'). Who knows? But I realised quite early on that in America there were no safety-nets. In the UK, however obnoxious, I had some credit with those whose patience I regularly tested to destruction and beyond. I was tolerated, even at my worst. I might be a drunken son of a bitch, but I was their son of a bitch. People felt responsible for me; some even owed me for favours done while sober. There was always a wagon to climb back on. In America, there was nothing: just disgrace, freefall and a one-way ticket to Skid Row, the closed ward, or the mortuary. The absence of a net underneath me added a cutting-edge of riskiness to my drinking, nudging me over the brink on which I had been teetering for years. I felt, excitingly, that I was dicing with ruin (and, beyond that, the noseless one). I felt 'bad'; *homo MalcolmLowriensis*, living under my personal volcano. Looking back, I see it as the delusion of grandeur which is common with the terminal alcoholic – nothing existential, just another telltale symptom.

There were pressing difficulties of a humbler nature. Oddly, finding somewhere to drink convivially was one of them. Pasadena is a ribbon, stretched out on the five-mile length of Colorado Boulevard (the same route that the Rose Parade takes every New Year's Day; I watched this grotesque festival in 1983, in blinding sunshine, with a thumping head and a parched throat). The whole of LA County is constructed for the automobile (and before that, the horse; and before that, the lizard).

One of the problems for a pedestrian drinker like myself was that there were no bars within walking distance. I had, as yet, no car. A new colleague had sold me an English Raleigh, a young fogey's bicycle, complete with handlebar basket. If I wanted to drink, I would have to pedal for it. Or, as a last resort, drink in my apartment. I longed for London's ubiquitous pubs.

The only drinking I could find within cycling distance (at least, cycling-back distance) was, as it turned out, Pasadena's sole gay bar. It had the unlovely name, Nardi's (half naff, half sordid, as I merrily thought). It was not what I would have chosen, but that was how the chips fell. On the any-port-in-a-storm principle, I adopted Nardi's as my local. Drinking went on till 2am, the legal closing time in California. Thereafter, a hard-core of survivors would adjourn to someone's apartment.

I had never explored gay sex. But it was the only thing on offer at Nardi's. And, in a way, it seemed to fit in with my current Baudelairean sense of self. A new, dangerous road to explore. In fact, it turned out to be baffling rather than adventurous. After one heavy night I awoke from blackout to find myself slumbering alongside an African-American whose name, I dimly remembered, was Richard. We were both partly undressed. My hand brushed against his penis (accidentally, as I trust), and felt nothing there (I'm fairly sure this was not an hallucination). His Johnson had been cut off, amputated. Perhaps it was a preliminary to a sex-change operation.

It was just as well things went no further. Aids was reaching epidemic levels in southern California, although, in 1983, no one was entirely clear as to what the new disease was. I would almost certainly have contracted the virus had I carried on as I was then doing for a night or two more.

It was the morning of 11 February 1983. I had a monster hangover. The phone rang: it was Richard's parole officer phoning up to make sure he was home and not violating his curfew. (What, I vaguely wondered, had he been in for? Penis chopping?) I made my ultra-English excuses and left. I emerged into blinding early-morning sunlight among the palms and skuzzy bungalows of western Altadena – Rodney King territory, as would be famous, eight years later. If Officer Koon had been going at me all night with his mighty Kevlar truncheon I could not have felt more bruised.

This, as I walked down the interminable miles of Marengo Avenue, was the end of my night and the morning of clarity. Was this what it had come to? All that grind, the degrees, the books read and the books written? Holding the penile stump of someone I barely knew, in a god-forsaken California ghetto in a sun-baked country where I didn't belong?

I would have one more drunk: the final test. Me versus my alcoholic destiny. It would be no half-hearted affair. I bought two bottles of cheap California champagne and a large, two-quart flagon of Gallo's even cheaper Chardonnay (as back-up, when the fizz ran out and one's palate had lost its discriminating edge: the alcoholic mind at work). This last stash was taken back in the basket of my Raleigh and consumed – gulped – in my apartment. I can taste the saccharin-acrid Gallo's now. I was, finally, a wino. End of the line, Ma.

Of course, my tolerance was shot. I needed a lot less than I had bought to do the trick. But, somehow, I finished it all off (never let it be said a Sutherland left an empty flagon). I blacked out early. When I came to, all the furniture had been rearranged. I never did find out which fairies had done it.

I awoke to a different world. The sun had gone in. For ever, as it seemed. Southern California was now experiencing record-breaking rains (some damned weather record is always being broken over there). The Queen of England, no less, was visiting a West Coast sodden all the way from Vancouver to Baja California. Storm systems were backed up like a Venetian blind, all the way to Japan, waiting to sweep in and dump their load on me and my monarch.

Pacific storms are different from Britain's 'soote shoures'. They are made up of heavy drops, widely spaced. It is, somehow, a harder rain and can deposit up to three inches a day (a third of the annual rainfall in a dry year). The downpour triggers mudslides. Less dramatically, but more dangerously, the patina of tyre-rubber and grease on the freeways, baked for months on end by the desert sun, is moistened into pure slick. Withered windscreen-wipers peel and smear. People get nervous and short-tempered. In short, the Golden State turns and looks ugly when it rains. Apocalyptically so. The great flood, they say, will be more destructive than the great earthquake, 'the big one'.

Alcoholics are always on the lookout for their 'objective correlative' (as T.S. Eliot called it). My internal works were as turbulent as the end-of-the-world weather. I emerged from my bout with the Gallo brothers in the grip of agonising withdrawal. Uneven heartbeat, panic attacks, dislocation of time (minutes became hours; days passed as eye-blinks before I could even pretend to do any work). I was sweaty and chilled at the same time. I was hearing voices, experiencing visual phenomena (jagged zigzags of light out of the corner of my eyes), afflicted by paranoid persecution-fantasy in public places (Why *were* people looking at me that way? Did they know?); ravenous, nauseous, anorexic by turns.

It is a state of mind in which banal events take on the portentousness of symbol or prophetic sign. I walked, pelted with rain, past the local supermarket, Louis Foods, and saw genteel senior citizens, as they always did in the morning, rooting in the skips ('dumpster diving') for the perishables which Californian state law obliges retailers to discard after 24 hours. The old gents civilly made way for the old ladies among them to take first pick of yesterday's sandwiches. It was, in my suicidal frame of mind, an incredibly depressing sight. And there was a kind of *de te fabula* aspect to it – how long before I was there, shuffling through the garbage with the geezers?

I found myself, at mid-day, in my office at Caltech, shuddering like a holed fox. I had forced down some food, at that incredibly early lunch-time the Americans like, around 11.30am. Chilli con carne (something warm, a distant maternal voice told me, would be cheering). I can taste and see it now: white onion, lying like maggots, on tongue-scorching red sauce. It lay in my stomach like a pocketful of billiard balls.

It was drink or not drink time. And the next drink, I feared, would be decisive. A one-way ticket into the dark – goodbye high-functioning; hello dumpster diving. I was very frightened. After a riffle through the *Yellow Pages*, I phoned up AA – some forgotten Samaritan had once told me about the helpline. I was not, as I expected, put on hold. After two rings, my details were taken (most importantly: 'When did you have your last drink?). Ten minutes later, I was told to go to a nearby street-corner rendezvous. I would be met. Right on the button, a nice guy, Ken H. (market-gardener and recovering alcoholic), rolled by in his pickup. There were cacti sticking up in the back of his truck.

I was subjected to what I would later recognise as a hail of AA patter as Ken drove me off to a lunchtime speaker meeting in San Marino. It was my introduction to the wacky world of So-Cal AA. On the 'Where were you when Kennedy was shot?' principle, I can remember the event vividly. It was classic dusty church hall, stale cookies, bitter coffee, high-pressure *bonhomie*. There were lots of sober retirees (some there, I suspect, on the 'never turn down a free lunch' principle).

A smartly uniformed Hispanic security guard (from the Huntington!) called Mañuel spoke about his year's sobriety as he 'took his cake'. Before coming to AA, Mañuel had been 'homicidal and suicidal'. Life was good now. He was a happy menial Mañuel. Try as I might, I could not 'identify' with the success stories of uniformed men who opened doors for me. Drunk I might be, but I wanted more from life than that. Snobbery is the last thing to be eroded by alcohol.

Ken, who was not as dumb as I (with my Marie Antoinette prejudices) took him to be, perceived that it wasn't working. That same evening, he chauffeured me on to a Participation meeting. This was something else: a 'closed' (alcoholics only), all-Californian, male affair with the rueful name 'The Wheel Grippers' (life, in other words, is one damned traffic jam). There were no African-Americans, no 'minorities': this was redneck, with a bit of grubby white-collar. The tone of the discussion was extravagantly macho, amoral and incorrigibly racist.

Ken, himself, was a changed guy in this company, bubbling over with stories about nights in whorehouses, jail-time, fights. There were several ex-cons there and a couple of still-serving cops. One of the men in blue (sworn to 'serve and protect') cheerfully told how he had shot gooks in Korea and how he'd like the fuck to go out in the streets now with his M16 and clean things up. Give him a few good homicidal maniacs and it would take three weeks, 'max'. There was some demur from those who suspected that they might be on the receiving end. But hell, this was a place where you could speak your mind.

Another Wheel Gripper, Slim, announced that he'd just come from Bob's Big Boy. He was completely broke and knew, when he told the cashier he couldn't pay for his double-double burger, that she'd just tell him to hand over his driving licence. Which, of course, he'd handed over at Burger King the day before! 'You're *weird*,' was all she could say. Not worth calling the law for seven dollars and three cents.

Slim was currently living in his (uninsured, of course) wreck of a car. His address, as he liked to joke, was the same as the licence number. In California, your automobile says everything about you. The fleet outside the meeting ranged from Cadillacs to ten-year old 'compacts' (the SoCal equivalent of Del-boy's Robin Reliant), Slim's mobile home and my own Raleigh bicycle (I, alone, had no wheel to grip: just sit-up-and-beg handlebars).

All the Grippers seemed to have, and love, guns (something else I didn't have and don't love). All, even the married ones, seemed to have 'girlfriends'. 'What the fuck, this isn't a training for the *priesthood*,' Pat O. later explained to me. And, he advised me – good buddy that he was – that meetings were a perfect cover for fooling around: Adulterers Anonymous. In America, everything has old-world ethnic roots, if you dig deep enough. In the Wheel Grippers, it was 100-per-cent-proof Irish. This was a paddy pub with no beer.

Some of the Grippers were business successes. At least one had a private plane. There was a surgeon who, though sober, still couldn't keep his hands off his secretaries (much bawdy mirth), but had, thank God, managed *not* to raid the drugs cabinet for six weeks ('Way to go!'; small round of applause). All the Wheel Grippers spoke in that fluent, hard, inventive vernacular which sounded as if it had been scripted for Jack Webb 30 years before. A Sergeant Friday, however, with the morals of James Ellroy. 'I used to feel guilty about what I put my woman through; but *shit*, she could have split any time. She just hung around to watch me croak' – this from a speaker who, on getting sober, promptly divorced 'the bitch'. That was his goddamned moment of clarity. There was only one thing that united this group and brought them together: they didn't drink any more. It was enough.

I gravitated away from the hard men to an older, gentler man. Harry S. had dried out twice: once for 13 years, once for 17. He was an oldtimer twice over. He had several marriages and a number of careers behind him. He had flown B24 bombers in the postwar period and had seen a bit of real action in Korea. He was still nostalgic for those glory days (happy drinking days, too). He had subsequently been a PanAm pilot, before disqualifying himself. He had been an insurance salesman – almost impossible to drink yourself out of *that* job. And, if you were a nice guy (which he was), it was easy to scrape by. He was, like Willy Loman, 'well liked'. But he got less energetic with age, and now he was rather hopelessly peddling air-exchangers to small businesses wanting to solve their smoke-filled-room problems. (He should try selling to AA, I suggested: no cash, he bleakly replied. And, he might have added, the air-exchangers didn't work all that well, anyway.)

Harry S. was a variety of Californian I grew familiar with in AA. Professional life was one long quick-change act. One year they would be a schoolteacher, the next a fireman, and the year after that, having been ordained in a shack somewhere, a preacher. Rolling, tumbling through life. As someone who had been in the one professional groove, man and boy, I was constantly amazed by my fellow drunks' wild CVs. At Speaker meetings, I got to know born-again Christian ladies who had, within the memory of some of those present, been full-on strippers (the mind ran riot). I recall a former veterinarian who was now selling 'affordable caskets' (discount coffins). The commonest change was those who had been rich, sometimes very rich, who were now living in the weeds in the canyons, or in some crummy halfway house.

This chameleon-like ability to switch, in the blink of an eye, from career to career, lifestyle to lifestyle, was one of the reasons that, as they liked to say in SoCal AA, 'it works'. In a world of constant metamorphosis, what was strange about being a hopeless drunk one week and a sober success-story the next? California is, at root, an immigrant culture where your past is so far away geographically as to be lost: dropped off and forgotten like the fuel stages on a rocket. The past was simply what got you here. Start now. And start often.

Harry attached himself to me as I did to him. He needed to pass on his message to preserve his own sobriety (this is the rationale of the Twelfth Step – carrying the message to the alcoholic who still suffers). AA duty apart, Harry was genuinely nice, with a kind of burned-out wisdom about life. He longed to save enough cash from his air-exchangers to sail a yacht (and his third wife) round the world. Which, I think, he later did. The last postcard I received from him was from somewhere in South America.

Over my first weeks of sobriety Harry vaguely sponsored me. Not very successfully (he was far too deferential about my degrees, my big salary, my $10-words). But just drinking coffee with him was fun therapy. He was a repository of sagacious truth about drink, drinkers and drunks. You can never tell who will make it, he would say, having watched AA at work for three decades. Often the successes were the apparent deadbeats. The down-at-heels, bums, the ones who turned up still drunk and bleary. Those who looked like really good prospects – the bright-eyed, eager, clever ones – would most likely flame out. He was right. It was a lottery. Do not despair, as St Augustine said, one thief was saved: do not presume, one thief was damned. Which thief was I?

I wanted something more than Harry could give and found it at a Speaker meeting where a large bearded alcoholic, with an eerie resemblance to the young Burl Ives, came up to chat during the coffee-break. Peter C. was one of the more remarkable comrades I encountered in the fellowship. He was a freelance carpet-layer, with a PhD in archaeology from Harvard. He had recently become interested in folklore and was writing a book on werewolves (it was published during my second year of sobriety, and remains, I understand, the most scholarly work on that much-travestied subject). Peter C. came from a fundamentalist German *émigré* community infused with iron-hard Calvinism and grim depression (close members of his family had committed suicide, I later discovered). His mind was profoundly theological. He took to AA like a fish to water and enjoyed high-priest status in the groups he attended. He attended a lot: five meetings a week, minimum.

I am inclined to judge Peter C. as the most impressively learned man I have met – even though my professional life has been passed among a community of academic wiseacres and smart-ass operators. But, in that paradoxical Californian way, reassuring veins of philistinism ran through his superfine intellect; like fat in streaky bacon. He had a huge arsenal of guns. One of his greatest pleasures (in sobriety) was donning his leathers to ride with a motorcycle gang. Not for Peter C. the sherry-laden gentilities of the senior common room.

With Peter C. as my Virgil (he suggested the analogy) I attended some 'satin-sheet' meetings in Hollywood – not to his taste; but he appreciated I was, only three months in Tinseltown, still something of a rubberneck. It beat Disneyland. At one Beverly Hills meeting, I found myself actually sitting next to a 'star' (OK, a once-upon-a-time star), Aldo Ray. I had seen him, as a boy, in such steaming romances as *God's Little Acre* (with its just off-screen act of fellatio, which provoked much wondering speculation in Colchester in 1958) and *Miss Sadie Thomson*. In those days, the 1950s, Aldo was built like Adonis, had an Astroturf crew-cut, and a voice like a slow cement-mixer.

Now only the gravelly voice remained. Aldo had, 30 years on, come down in the world. He was flabby, shabby and beat-up by life. There were no safety-nets for screen actors any more than for college professors. He had, a few years ago, been offered his 'star' on the pavement of Hollywood Boulevard but couldn't come up with the $3,000 they charged for that tawdry honour (if he'd had even that little cash – chump-change for real Hollywood players – his creditors would have fallen on him like vultures). I noticed, during the Seventh Tradition, that when everyone else pitched in their dollar, Aldo merely fumbled in his pocket and passed the basket on no fuller than it was when it came to him.

As he munched resolutely on somebody's birthday cake in the coffee-break, he reminisced – for the millionth time, one suspected – about 'Bogey', with whom he'd worked on *We're No Angels*.

A luckier alcoholic than Aldo, Bogart (legend has it) died with the famous last words, 'I should have stuck to Bourbon.' Aldo died himself in 1991. No last words are recorded; nor whether the poor slob died sober or with Bourbon on his breath. I've often wondered why the hawkers you see on the pavement of Sunset Boulevard don't sell the AA *Big Book* rather than those tacky *Star Map* guides.

Peter C., who appointed himself my spiritual as well as my temporal guide, favoured a local AA meeting – the '77', a low-bottom haven. No satin sheets for 77. It was ostentatiously squalid: the kind of meeting which took pride in its coffee tasting like battery acid; in the Maxwell House jar-top ashtrays (always overflowing) and the torn, Rexine-covered chairs, salvaged from some local refuse dump. Its core membership were sober bums, halfway-house inmates, men rebounding from unemployment or prison, and quite a few women who had given up what they called 'prostituting' (clearly because they no longer had even the minimal physical requirements that line of work takes). While he held on, one poor sod attended along with the oxygen tanks that were all that kept him from death by lung cancer or emphysema. It didn't stop the rest of the group smoking volcanically. The 77 was regularly dropped in on by slumming West Side drunks. I recall one, an actor who I still regularly see on TV re-runs. He was astonishingly eloquent about how, that very morning, he had woken up to find a SWAT team outside his apartment. His no-good, drugged-up son, had robbed some store. I didn't much like the 77 zoo. But Peter C. thought it was good to rub my nose in *echt* alcoholism. He may have been right.

Why, I've often wondered, does AA work so well in LA? It thrives differently (and in my view less well) elsewhere. In New Hampshire, I found the meetings oppressively private; infused to the point of moral implosion with a New England puritan shame. On a practical level, it was hard to find out where they were being held (no one wanted to proclaim their sin: the big scarlet letter had to be hidden). One felt like an early Christian in the catacombs. In the South, I am told, there are meetings in the hills where you have to hand in your gun at the door. Doubtless, there are meetings in Texas where you hitch your horse.

But in southern California the dominant motif is a kind of freewheeling zaniness. There are as many kinds of AA meeting as there are churches (every one of which is its own denomination, with its own distinctive ritual and theodicy). The devolved organisation of AA thrives on the West Coast. AA/LA has heavy-smoker, moderate-smoker and non-smoker meetings, closed gay meetings, sex-addict meetings, meetings where women knit and exchange pie recipes, cyclist meetings which get together and celebrate their Spandex-lean sobriety on mountain peaks, biker meetings where the un-tattooed enter at risk of their lives, meetings that muster on the fringe of pop concerts (Grateful Dead were a particular favourite), meetings that hang out in gyms and muscle themselves into the right frame of mind (there was, though I never went to it, a scientists' AA at Caltech; you probably needed a PhD in theoretical physics to 'qualify').

The relatively small range of meetings I patronised worked for me. I got sober and found sobriety to be a strange experience. The days, once a frantic race against closing time, were suddenly long and empty. What to do? I couldn't drive for a couple of months. My nerves were too jangled. And, when I took to the roads again, I was as nervous as a cat. I had lost boldness with my drinking habit. I was a shy automobilist. I also discovered, as many recovering drunks do, that alcohol had for years masked chronic depression, which I had now to deal with.

I was healthy and quickly got fit (work and workouts were something with which I could fill the empty hours). I discovered that I was, although not the genius that I once thought, competently good at my job now that I could give it my clear-headed attention. Slowly but inexorably a career began to take shape again. California is the land of the fresh start. My Caltech colleagues had noted my drunkenness but they noted, equally, my mended ways and approved. The job offer came and I accepted. My family took the risk and joined me. Unwise, some would have said; but the bet paid off. I was, it seemed, the saved thief.

Unlike many alcoholics, I had no craving to drink again. Indeed, within a few months, whole days would pass in which I would not think of alcohol once. And, with this indifference, my need for AA diminished. The fellowship had saved me, but I didn't want to hold on to that lifebelt all my life. I had, I felt, served my time. AA gurus (particularly the relentless Peter C.) warned me that if you 'go out' you *will* relapse. I haven't nor, frankly, do I think I will.

I did, however, have one more whirl with AA/LA; more specifically with its undergrowth of juvenile mutations. I know about the groups for teen addicts not because I was myself ever young and stoned in LA, but because my son was. Addiction was, I suppose, my legacy to him, his patrimony; like alcoholic father, like addict son.

Jack arrived in southern California to join me, after I straightened out in 1983. He was then nine. By the age of 14 he had a bottle of vodka stashed in his school locker and was using any number of substances. Fondly, his parents knew nothing of this. There were suspicious empty sachets in trouser-pockets tossed in the wash, and the usual array of signs – red eyes, inflamed lips and nostrils, poor grades, small sums of money regularly disappearing (and, sometimes, larger sums), a taste for thunderous and repetitious heavy metal (I still hate the sound of Led Zeppelin). But we didn't see anything too sinister. Hell, he was only a teenager, and, if he was teenager, and if he was 'dabbling', that was a routine part of the Californian educational syllabus.

Then, of course, the unavoidable thing. He attempted suicide. It was a well-planned attempt (by hanging, not firearm, thank God). Self-destruction is, one discovered, the major cause of death among young Californians under the age of 16 (when they can take to the road, racing like lemmings to the cliff). He left – or intended to leave – a heart-wrenching note saying that he confidently expected a happy family reunion in the hereafter. But that things on earth were, currently, unbearable. He had touched bottom, aged 15, and wanted out. It was drink 'n' drugs that did it. That, and the usual adolescent sexual confusion.

It was, in a sense, his youth that saved him. Because he *was* under 16 he had no rights. One of the most interesting features of the West Coast medical industry is the 'closed-treatment facility' – sanatoriums for the under-age. Jack was referred, within 12 hours of his suicide attempt, to an adolescent unit at Ingleside (called, irreverently, 'Ingletraz' by its youthful inmates). Most of the kids had to be taken there kicking and screaming. He was still too shaken up to protest too much. No matter if he had. He was under 16.

Ingletraz was hugely expensive – $5,000 a week (picked up, for a month only, by my medical insurance). It was, none the less, value for money and had a good success-rate. There was one nurse per inmate, 24-hour CCTV surveillance, daily one-on-one meetings with therapists, and supervised 12 Step meetings three times a day. In the evening, these would be 'family' meetings, in which parents and siblings would be involved (this was the only time in my ten years in southern California that I had anything like intimate conversation with non-alcoholic Hispanics and African-Americans: suffering parents, like me). The institution was organised on correctional-facility principles. The juvenile inmate arrived with no privileges at all, other than food and sleep. Good behaviour earned 'points'; these could be converted into 'air time' (the right to go outside and smoke), visitors or candy.

It was intense and – given the fact that most of the insurance coverage ran out after a month or so – necessarily short. The follow-up was AA, MA (Marijuana Anonymous) and NA (Narcotics Anonymous) – all of which have teenage chapters in LA. This system is highly interventionist and offensive to many liberals. It would have been offensive to me, had I been an idle observer of it. As it is, my judgment is tempered by the fact that places like Ingletraz work. I suspect one reason is the green-stick mendability of the young – if you intervene hard enough and at the right moment. Middle-aged drunks, like myself, need to be broken wholly before they can be reset. And they have to perform the operation themselves. It's different for the young. Screw civil rights and save the child, I say.

Even if he had not killed himself but had kept on drinking and using, Jack would certainly have come to a bad end very quickly. His three closest friends (fellow Led Zeppelin lovers) got wasted six months later in one of their girlfriends' houses. The parents, this being southern California, had guns around for the 'armed response' which you are warned about on every middle-class front lawn. After drinking and doping to toxic levels, for reasons they will doubtless never understand, two of the boys killed the three girls by shotgun ('Man, we *smoked* them all,' one of them wonderingly said later). The state prosecutor wanted the death penalty. They smoked them all; he would fry them all. But they were under 16 at the time of the crime and got life without parole. Two of them (the third plea-bargained his way out by giving evidence) will die in prison. Jack, I firmly believe, would have been with them but for Ingletraz.

As it is, he recovered. I followed his path through a maze of AA/MA/NA groups as strange to me as Mars. Meetings with more tattoos than a British battleship; valley girls, jumped-out gang members, designer-clad ex-junkies. It looked like fun. But if you're young, everything is fun. Even alcoholism. Life is less fun, but he is 12 years clean and sober.

'I have lost Los Angeles as a locale,' Raymond Chandler lamented in 1957, on moving to London. 'It is no longer the part of me it once was.' I lost my Los Angeles as well, when I returned to London after ten years in 1992. But I suppose, at least I hope, I brought LA/AA with me. I'll die an alcoholic, I know. But, hopefully, a sober one.

AUTHOR BIOGRAPHY

John Sutherland is Lord Northcliffe Professor of Modern English Literature at UCL, and a visiting professor at the California Institute of Technology. A recovering drunk, he is the author of many, many books.

Other books in the **FRONTLINES** series:

British Teeth
An excruciating journey from the dentist's chair to the
rotten heart of a nation
William Leith

The Strange World of Thomas Harris
Inside the mind of the creator of Hannibal Lecter
David Sexton

Funeral Wars
How lawyer Willie Gary turned a petty dispute about
coffins into a multi-million-dollar morality play
Jonathan Harr

Your Pedigree Chum
Like most dog-lovers, Missy's owners think she is irreplaceable –
and they are rich enough to do something about it
James Langton

Nurse Wolf & Dr Sacks
This is New York...a dominatrix and
a doctor share tales of the city
Paul Theroux

Also published by Short Books, **Short Lives:**

The Voice of Victorian Sex: Arthur H. Clough
Rupert Christiansen

The Boy Who Inspired Thomas Mann's
'Death in Venice': Wladyslaw Moes
Gilbert Adair

A Material Girl: Bess of Hardwick
Kate Hubbard

Inventor of the Disposable Culture:
King Camp Gillette
Tim Dowling

Last Action Hero of the British Empire:
Cdr John Kerans
Nigel Farndale

The Hungarian Who Walked to Heaven:
Alexander Csoma de Koros
Edward Fox

Discoverer of the Human Heart: William Harvey
Ronan Bennett

The Hated Wife: Carrie Kipling
Adam Nicolson